# WESTERN COWBOY POETRY

## An African American Perspective

*Sharon Carpenter*

iUniverse, Inc.
Bloomington

iUniverse books may be ordered through booksellers or by contacting:

iUniverse
1663 Liberty Drive
Bloomington, IN 47403
www.iuniverse.com
1-800-Authors (1-800-288-4677)

Because of the dynamic nature of the Internet, any Web addresses or links contained in this book may have changed since publication and may no longer be valid. The views expressed in this work are solely those of the author and do not necessarily reflect the views of the publisher, and the publisher hereby disclaims any responsibility for them.

Any people depicted in stock imagery provided by Thinkstock are models, and such images are being used for illustrative purposes only.

Certain stock imagery © Thinkstock.

ISBN: 978-1-4697-5567-0 (sc)
ISBN: 978-1-4697-5566-3 (hc)
ISBN: 978-1-4697-5565-6 (e)

Library of Congress Control Number: 2012902031

Printed in the United States of America

iUniverse rev. date: 4/5/2012

# CONTENTS

## Section 2:  Workin' It—Cowboy Hustlin' and Rustlin'

## Section 3:  Romancin'—Cowboy Love Stories

## Section 4:  Our Values—A Cowboy Life Perspective

# Introduction

*Western Cowboy Poetry* presents a look at the history of the American frontier through the eyes of some of its forgotten explorers, the African Americans who headed west seeking freedom and opportunity. The poetry contained was designed for raising awareness through an entertaining venue as a performing poet speaking aloud to diverse audiences.

*Section One: The Journey and Contributions—A Historic Perspective* presents an interpretation of what life may have been like for those who sought a place to live in freedom from slavery. It delivers a perspective on the challenges they encountered in the Wild West, where they strove to acquire autonomy, to work, and to live in family units instead of being pulled away from each other, sold as slaves to different owners.

There were many African Americans who gained renown as contributors to western history. Consider Bridget ("Biddy") Mason, an African American female born in 1818 who won freedom from slavery for herself and her daughters through the US District Court of Appeals. Initially she worked as a nurse and midwife, and ultimately, she became recognized as a successful entrepreneur, philanthropist, and one of the first black, female, wealthy landowners in Los Angeles. She provided food and shelter for people of all races and, with her son-in-law's support, established the first church for blacks in Los Angeles, the African Methodist Episcopal Church. *(Reference:* Epic Lives: One Hundred Black Women Who Made A Difference, *edited by Hessie Carey Smith)*

Another renowned black woman who had an impact on life out west was Mary Fields, a.k.a. "Stagecoach Mary." Mary attained notoriety for her apparent fearlessness as a stagecoach driver, horseback rider, and gunslinger. One of the first African American female mail carriers, she was also a former mission worker and restaurant owner, where her attributes as a caregiver were eminent. Although Mary had a reputation as a whiskey drinker and cigar smoker, she was considered a celebrity in Cascade, Montana, where the mayor officially authorized her to drink in the all-male saloons. (*Reference:* Black Frontiers, A History of African American Heroes in the Old West *by Lillian Schlissel*)

Other significant contributors that later became notorious include the "Buffalo Soldiers" of the 9th and 10th Cavalry Regiments—the first black segment of the United States military during the Civil War and post-Civil-War era. They were renowned for their fortitude, strong sense of duty, and commitment to the protection of others. Not only were they warriors, but they were also instrumental in the growth, safety, and expansion of the West. They built roads and telegraph lines, provided protection for cattle drivers, staffed railroad crews, drove stage coaches, delivered the mail, and more. They have been honored with their own museum, Buffalo Soldiers National Museum; with Congressional Medals of Honor; and with films such as *Glory*. (*References:* The Forgotten Heroes: The Story of The Buffalo Soldiers, *by Clinton Cox*; Cathy Williams: From Slave to Female Buffalo Soldier, *by Phillip T. Tucker; www.ushist.com/buffalo-soldiers.htm.*)

After the Civil war, freed African American slaves did not automatically become landowners. Many continued as farmers (called "sharecroppers") for former slave owners. They were able to work, yet they did not receive monetary compensation; the expectation was that they would repay a share of everything they raised as farmers in exchange for food, shelter, and clothing. Ultimately, this resulted in perpetual debt. In time, thanks to members of the community such as Benjamin Singleton, a former slave from Tennessee, word spread about job opportunities in the North that would lead to obtaining land in the West. Singleton was committed to the establishment of a community of two hundred African American families. As a result of his diligence and the efforts of others, communication about opportunities occurred. Ultimately, many blacks left the South to pursue better lifestyles in places such as Nebraska and Oklahoma, and eventually established large African

American communities. Among the most famous were Taft, Langston, and Boley in Nebraska and Oklahoma, and Nicodemus and Dunlap in Kansas. (*Reference:* Black Frontiers, A History of African American Heroes in the Old West, *by Lillian Schlissel*)

*Section Two: Workin' It—Cowboy Hustlin' and Rustlin'* imagines what the work experience may have been like many years after the war ended, based on historical findings. Even prior to the Civil War, some African Americans had migrated to the West. Notably, of the approximately thirty thousand cowboys who were cattle drivers, one out of four was African American. Inclement weather such as severe blizzards, dust storms, or wind gusts at times resulted in devastating losses of cattle for these ranchers. In 1886 a severe blizzard destroyed thousands of cattle. This resulted in drastic losses to ranchers in Kansas, the Dakotas, Nebraska, Arizona, and Colorado, with a significant impact on the African American community. *Section Two* also alludes to a variety of experiences that were appealing to some African Americans during that era, and that many enjoy today. These include branding cattle, bronco riding, rounding up and taming horses, as well as tending to ranches and livestock either for landowners landowner. (*References:* Cowboys, The Real Story of Cowboys and Cattlemen, *by Royal B. Hassrick*; Bill Pickett: Rodeo-Ridin' Cowboy, *by Andrea D. Pinkney*)

*Section Three: Romancin'—Cowboy Love Stories* aims to entertain by describing interactions between friends and possible intimacies among men and women in the West. Viewpoints in this section include contemporary as well as historic sentiment. What may romance have been like for a female in love with a renowned cattle rustler? How might one connect with others in a dance hall, after completing a long day out on the plains?

*Section Four: Our Values—A Cowboy Perspective* comprises poems that reflect values that African American cowhands may have acquired while enjoying the lifestyle of a cowhand in the West. These values are addressed from an introspective viewpoint that captures strong work ethic, integrity, spirituality, socialization, and autonomy, as well as commitment to impart sustainable improvements in the form of caring for others and for the environment.

# Acknowledgments

**Elizabeth Collins,** beloved foster mom whose demonstrated commitment to living for Christ, through her daily life, prayer, and thanksgiving, is what enabled Sharon to accept Christ as her personal Savior at age seventeen. Her support, influence, and encouragement are what prompted the focus beyond life experiences as a foster child. It was foundational to the gradual realization Sharon acquired that it is not what happened to you, although it may be heartrending, but how you respond to the situation that impacts the quality of your life.

**Joel Hayes,** "the father of Georgia Cowboy Poetry," founder of Douglas County's Poetry Writers Group, Douglasville, Georgia, and partner in *Chuck Wagon Cooking*. According to Paul Mason, Senior Pastor at Central Baptist Church, Joel, a deacon and leader, "has been uniquely endowed with the gift of philosophy and poetic verse. In his poetry there is embedded a person of the soil with a profound message. Wit and wisdom go hand in hand. All that he pens points to a heart of love and adoration for the Lord and for his fellow man." It was Joel Hayes who introduced Sharon to cowboy poetry and encouraged her to not only write but also to perform.

**Tylene Nikkole,** Sharon's daughter who insisted her mother publish what she had created for a variety of performances throughout the years. Tylene pointed out the value as a legacy it would bring not only to her daughters and granddaughters from a storytelling perspective, but shared insight to others from a unique entertaining style about African American cowboy life and their contributions.

**Charlie Holloway**, author of *Old Saddles & Good Advice*, performing cowboy poet, and also renowned for his chuck wagon cooking. Charlie always encouraged Sharon to publish the poetry and he assisted in "getting butts in the seats" at the cowboy gatherings. Both he and Joel imparted history of the cowboy lifestyle. She was invited on several occasions to join them on their wagon-trail events as a performing poet.

**Peggy McColl**, international best-selling author who provided inspiration and guidance through her coaching program and her lifestyle as a caregiver on how to expend the time, energy, and passion to share the book as a viable outreach to others.

# SECTION ONE
## The Journey and Contributions— A Historic Perspective

# The Exodus

You ask to hear my story
Of what it was like
Way back when,
As a weary sojourner,
On dusty trails
Westward:
The destiny of men.

It was a dream for many
(As well as for me)
To find a plot of land
And live in tranquility.
To settle upon plains, fertile with wheat,
Where we could grow our own crops
And have plenty to eat.

A place where we could lay
Our weary heads
And have big families
And our own adobe sheds.
A place where we could nestle in
And be respected—
Be human.

They told us land out West
Was for the takin';
All it required, they said,
Was willingness and gumption.
After the War, they beckoned us to come.
"Till the land," they said,
"And settle down some."

They told stories about the land o' plenty
Of golden wheat, of warm bright sun,
Of spacious places
Under the heavens.
They told stories about work galore,
And how the payoff was beyond
What we ever dreamed we could score!

Some of us were skeptical, 'tis true,
But the stalwart proved valiant
All the way through.
We turned in our sharecroppers' tools,
Packed up our gunny sacks—such as they were—
And hastened to Mississippi,
To Dallas, to Omaha, and more.

Few were fortunate to hop a ride
On a barge down the Mississippi.
The bulk of us treaded the riverbank
To Arkansas, to Texas
And other westward places,
Trudging for days and months
Toward the land of golden acres.

But hope lay light upon our hearts;
So much so that we felt not the burden of the sacks
We carried so ardently upon tired backs.
For the promise was given to us, you see,
To follow this course to victory—
This course that led to our own place,
Where we could build with God's good grace.

We nurtured the dream within our breasts
As we lay upon hard ground

To take our rest.
Our feet were cracked, sore,
And swollen with pain,
But our hearts fluttered freely
With the vision of gain.

The journey over plain and mountain
Took us through much consternation.
We encountered tough soil
Embedded with rock
That stubbornly refused to yield
To our worn hands
As they kneaded those western lands.

We suffered cold, bleak winters
And long, dreary nights.
Summers brought us dust,
So frightfully thick,
That blinded us along the way;
Yet, we were determined
To find destiny's gateway.

Many scorned us, who saw us come
Ragged and nasty with filth;
But our hearts remained light with the vision
Of our homesteads—
Free in spacious places
Where the sun shines, warm and golden in its crest,
And where we, as weary travelers can finally rest.

Thus, we journeyed
Without a mumblin' word
Despite the obstacles we faced;
Small price to pay

For children of God's grace
Now granted the freedom to live happily
In a promised land of plenty.

## The Blizzard of 1886—A Runaway's Perspective

It was ere the blizzard of '85,
I'd been a plottin'
'Bout three seasons
How I was gonna stay alive.
I reckoned if I endured the cattle trail,
Freedom at the end oughta prevail.

I don't know if you ever done a cattle run;
Ain't always a heap of fun.
Why 'em cows, stubborn as a cuss,
Can put up an awfully big fuss,
As cantankerous as they wanna be—
They don't always listen to me.

They ain't the smartest things in creation!
Why, it takes total damnation
To get 'em back on course
Once they stray.
It's like pluckin' cotton
To get 'em back on the way!

My life as a cowpoke is always on the line
As I run after their wayward behinds.
Naw, don't make me chase 'em cows
Through the brambles and rows—
Could be from sunup to midday ere I get 'em free;
Shucks, may as well be a-fightin' for my own liberty!

Like I said, I'd been a schemin'
'Bout three seasons now,
How I was gonna get my freedom somehow.
The plains was wide open, far as I could see;
Surely there was a way to get onto liberty!
So I set out as part of a cattle drive
To do whatever it took to stay alive.

That was the oddest fall season
I'd ever saw, I reason:
Though it started out nice and slow
Then, next thing you know—wind and snow
Was whirlin' us up, down, and all around,
Like we were nothin' but pasty dough!

Saw many froze as death's wintry fury
Hurled cattle and cowpokes, trying to bury us
'Twixt Dakota peaks, Arizona gullies, and Texas plains—
Thought we'd never see calmer days again!
Yet, oblivious was I of a doomsday plight,
I was determined to prevail,
For freedom was at the end of the cattle trail!

Lost four whole fingers through that cold blast,
Yet sallied on, I, through to the last.
After servitude, I refused to be lost,
I stood undaunted by a pitiless frost.
What was more intolerable: the white death,
Or to face, as a runaway, the foreman's wrath?

Would I make it? Who could tell?
To me, the odds were equal to see:
Either freedom at the end of the trail,
Or eternal freedom I would hail.

Didn't matter at all to me,
For I was in pursuit of liberty!

## Buffalo Soldier—On Acceptance

And is there a tale to be told
Of why we were so fearless and so bold,
Commended for our chivalry—
When what we longed,
What we dreamed,
Was to be esteemed, honored,
As decent human beings?

Is there a tale to spin
As we strutted
Through endless parades
And countless drills,
Applauded for our disciplined focus—
When what we sought
Was freedom from injustice?

Is there a tale to proclaim
While we lay in filth
And decrepit surroundings months on end,
Without wives, families, or friends—
Yet revered for our dignified demeanor
And respected for our contribution,
No matter the consequence?

Why did we stand tall,
Despite confrontations,
Not stooping to loot or to carouse?
We were set on a new day
Where we could proudly display

The virtues of soldiering: duty-bound
To ensure safety for others, no matter the town?

Here's the story we tell:
Energized by the quest
To be wage-earners, literate, and respected,
To no longer be ostracized and rejected,
But hailed as honorable and true,
Distinguished for going beyond
What the ordinary soldier would do.

So here's our tale.
Freedom is priceless;
You must stay the course,
No matter how elusive it may be.
Some say the duties of a buffalo soldier
Enabled us all to live safely
And free.

## Buffalo Soldier—The Homefront

I stand atop the stairs
Watchin' him head off
To God knows where
Wonderin' if it's true
What they say
'Bout the cavalry
And the ole red, white, and blue.
Could it mean a better livin'?

Where earnin' your keep
Can be more than sharecroppin'?
But what if he never comes back?
Or they treat him harshly

And he gets off track?
Broken, so disappointed,
Destroyed by the futility of hope
'Cause some things don't seem to take shape
No matter how hard you set the stake.

How will this end?
Will this be the last embrace?
Will he ever come back to this place?
I miss him even now, and
The dust ain't settled.
Such a hard way he takes for me;
How my heart aches
For his company.

Get on wit' what you must do
Don't tarry, my beloved.
Hopin', prayin' for only the best,
Trustin' God to keep and sustain,
Alas! Steady I'll be at the homestead,
True to him I'll stay,
Longin' for that reunion,
Where we'll never more part company.

# Buffalo Soldier—The Legacy

Some of them
Were raring to do
Whatever it takes
To make a difference
For their kinfolk
Left behind
In nearly every state.

Fighting just seemed a natural thing;
Deciding which side leads to winning
Was the decision wrestled through.
Some chose the North,
Others struck out toward the South,
Never dreaming of loss:
All was aiming to conquer,
No matter the cost.

Lines became blurred
As the struggle continued
On how best to be heard:
Commence fighting for freedom?
Or dub it a loss,
Or stay the course
To discovery of a new life source?

Ultimately, many tried and true
Fought valiantly and fearlessly
For me and for you.
Setting a path—broadening—
Never to defect to tunneled thinking
That wrought confinement in every way.
And so this breed fought
And attained for us a new day!

These heroes,
Whose songs were never sung,
Envisioned finally being "human."
These who dared step out for the unheard—
We owe them endless thanks
For the strides we have made
As we come up through the ranks.

So let's raise the banner high,
And remember that
Life's journey is about
What destiny grants us to fulfill.
To enable others to carry on,
Behind us,
Moving on over the hill.

## Buffalo Soldier—The Recruit

Hair kinky, skin dark as night,
Taut like canvas stretched over sinewy bones,
Clinging to pitchforks and twisted ropes,
Shoveling dashed dreams,
Tunneling, yet again,
To freedom.

Steeped in courage to defeat this plight
And undaunted by ghosts of failures past,
He dons the tattered uniform of a unique frontier
Where respect may be attained
Through chivalrous deeds
And absence of fear.

Eyes emboldened by the rigors of a slave's life,
The mantle worn with innocence and pride,
Chiseled by unrequited needs and a spark of hope.
He musters the fortitude to begin again:
The quest for respect
And a decent living.

He vows, "My country,
Wrong or right,
I deserve the chance to fight,

To preserve and to gain
The dignity that flourishes
When freedom reigns."

Thus he moves in this new space
Where escapades are won with God's grace.
Silently etching a memorial to his race,
For his deeds, unknown to some,
Rallied safety
And tranquility to thousands.

The toil of that laborious soul
That commenced ere the light of day
And extended far into the night—
Patroling the frontier
While protecting the mail,
Lest unseen danger prevail.

Thirteen dollars a month.
Clad oft-times in rotted clothes,
A broken horse to ride, defending others
Whilst his rights remained elusive—
Never respected or ever free—
Denied even as a soldier
In the U.S. Infantry.

Eons later, now we proclaim his fame
As truly a hero.
The treacherous path he trod:
Guarding stagecoaches and cattle drives,
Protecting railroad crews,
Helping others stay alive.

Diligent, a soldier in the U.S. Infantry.
One of the finest,
Brightest, shining stars
In pursuit of a hopeless feat:
To grasp the scepter
Where liberty and honor
And respectability meet.

## Biddy Mason—A Different Breed

She paid her dues
—The reason for her being—
She helped a heap of folk
With feedin', nursin', and churchin',
If'n it was needed.

Born a slave,
She traveled west,
From Mississippi to California
A step or two behind
Her Mormon master's wagon brigade—

Who was on a quest
For betterment
Along the frontier,
Pickin' up stakes
When the vision was near.

Biddy did a heap
Of birthin', breedin', and herdin'
She won her freedom
The hard way:
By the sweat of her brow—

Or so the courts say;
'Cause California, unlike back East,
Was a free state;
So being a slave,
Well, there wasn't much to debate.

Now when some get their freedom
They mosey on their way,
Leavin' it all behind;
But Biddy Mason
Was a different breed in her day.

She had a carin' heart,
Committed to helpin' others.
Wasn't nothin' too big or too small
Biddy wouldn't do
To help another hand get their due.

She had a hankerin'
To make it clear
Life was about sharin'
And givin' what was dear
Doin' what was a-needin' to be done.

Always helpin' families
Homestead in the ole West;
Get all settled
With food, shelter, work,
A real home, a real life, and real rest.

Yep! Biddy Mason
Was a different breed—
Carin' 'bout others—
Orphans and jailbirds too—

She even started a church
Where worship could be pure and true!

Smart as a whip, that Biddy,
She did a heap of cleanin' too.
Yet she managed to save,
To purchase property
Along the way.

Why that gal got fame
And she got fortune
As a landowner,
A mighty philanthropist
In her day.

Yessiree, Biddy
Was a different breed
The kind that every country
On this planet needs!

## Bartholomew

Bartholomew was a chap I knew
From runnin' herd now and again;
Quiet was he, hardly a peep,
Like someone always nearly asleep.
Sort of held his soul
Close to his chest,
And though he'd grin again and again,
None of us felt like we knowed him.

Now listen, 'cause I'm here to tell
Life on the prairie can be hell
With twists and turnin';

You just gotta know
Who to count on
When you's a-hurtin'
Or when the goin's slow.

So ol' Bart, all I knew,
He rode long and he rode hard,
Up and down old Mexico.
Heard he'd done a stint,
Down yonder in San Quent'—
For what I don't rightly know.
Y'all see, from what I knew,
He was as laid back as they go.

Can't begin to say much more,
Or how it came about,
Just knowed
While we was a-herdin'
The other day
We commenced to yakkin' 'bout folks
We'd knowed back in Slasterfield.

And you right in your thinkin'
If you a guessin',
I got to messin' in somethin'
I had no call to do,
But chasin' the time away,
Gives lots of latitude
For some display.

I got to yakkin'
'Bout a rowdy bunch
And a feller
From Slasterfield

That had no respect
For anyone—
Just did what he wanted to;
He had no accountin'.

He got in the way of a dame
Who dared this feller
By temptin' his fame.
Now some things you can do right;
Other things best left alone.
So, to try'n'a outwit some women ...
Best stay outta that zone.

Now I know y'all done heard the tale,
Of Samson and his lot—
Why, he went to prison
For boastin' quite a lot!
Indeed these tales is similar, you see,
'Cause this feller got caught up
In his adoration
For this gal named Bessie Lee.

She was far wittier than some,
And she held his love for ransom
To rob the next stagecoach
Comin' to town;
Thought Bessie Lee,
*How rare is love*
*Chasin' after me!*

Well, you probably done guessed the rest.
This guy was undaunted
By the request.
So to seal the deal,

Lovemakin' occurred
Under the moonlight.
Love struck his heart—

Indeed 'tis his blunder,
For the followin' day
He gave Bessie Lee the plunder.
And as he rode through the town
About dusk on that day,
Two cavalrymen in the shadows
Shot the feller above the heart
As he attempted to get away.

They dragged him to the prison
For seventeen years and a day.
And Bessie Lee?
She done reared a young'un
In the luxury of fine trappins',
For folks ne'er could prove,
Her wealth was from
This feller's wrappins'.

So there I was, a-carryin' on
About the treachery in women
On my mama's side,
When the feller connects the two,
And leans close by my ear,
And what he tells me
Makes my funnin' disappear—
This feller is my sister's son!

So it just goes to show:
While you can pick who you know,
You just might not be able

To pick your kin,
And you gotta watch what you say,
Or it sure may come back
To haunt you some day!

## Rodeo Clown

I paint up for every event
In reds, yellows, whites, and blues—
For I got an important task to do!
I don my britches
And put on my Stetson hat,
And 'fore I walk out the door,
Glue on my face an orange nose
To make sure I highlight more!

I draw lips from ear to ear
For the widest grin
Any bull could fear;
Then I step o'er the way
To the dusty grounds
Waiting for the time to come
To calm some bull down
With the antics I'll perform
As a rodeo clown.

Suddenly the gate
Is hoisted wide;
I'm summoned to the circle.
Eyes wide, cotton mouth,
My stance dug deep;
Lasso at my side,
I tilt my Stetson back
Toward the bull inside.

Mean, ugly, furious and a-snortin'
Toward me he comes,
Every breath puffed
With ominous air,
Eyes glinting with evil intention;
Aggravated by the noise
And the bronc rider's actions,
The bull stamps the ground—
Fed up with these distractions.

Toward me he comes,
Nostrils aflame with hate,
Thoroughly annoyed:
Time to put an end to this debate!
He lowers his head
And snorts obscenities in my direction,
I am now the new target
Of his unabated aggression.
I jingle my spurs and slap my sides
In exaggerated expression:
Somehow, I must distract this beast
Into a more peaceful suggestion.

Steady stand I, hands on hips,
Inviting the confrontation,
For I declare with pride
I'm the master
Of this bull's destination.
He glowers, I grunt,
And we sidle back and forth;
Sometimes I leap, sometimes I run,
Trying to convince him
It is better to have fun,

But he refuses my suggestion—
Rather, he attempts to clamp
Down on me and end my distraction.

As we prance, the bull's dance
Of death rings through.
One of us shall be no more,
And he's determined
To make this for me to be true.
But I proffer a milder sway,
A two-step back from death's
Trap door,
Beckoning now,
Through joviality and trickery—
The savage beast is no more.

Deafening applause
Lands on grateful ears;
I bow with grace,
One foot on the bull's neck,
While thanking destiny.
Mastered I this feat, again,
Without injury or loss of limb;
Acknowledging a higher call
Of the rodeo clown's angelic host,
Confirming it wasn't my time
To become a ghost.

## Toil in the Southwest

Work is work
No matter what you do,
Whether you're in the South
Or in Kalamazoo.

It don't come easy
For the likes of us;
We bend a bit lower
As our backs we thrust.

Ere sun-up
'Til long after dusk,
'Tis where you'll find
The majority of us:
Bendin' low,
Sweatin' hard,
A-workin' someone else's yard.

Whether plowin' the field
Or cleanin' the trough
Or drivin' a herd of cattle,
Stooped beneath our toils
We'll be,
Workin' hard—
No matter
The country.

## Trail Blazer

I look at your hands,
And wonder about you.
I gaze upon your sedentary stare,
And denote a confidence circumspect
Of inner peace,
The smile on your lips.

I study you,
Pondering your pose
As you lean serenely in repose.

I debate the evidence of calm
Displayed like garnish
In laugh lines around your mouth.

The mystique you carry in silence
Lends me to contemplate
What messages you've sent
By heavenly bodies that shine on
To a woman of your caliber
With auspicious aura.

What do you dream
As your thoughts
Rise higher than the skies?
What questions line your spirit,
Unresolved?
How astute is your inner ear
That extends beyond shadows and fear?

I look at you and study again
Your hands clasped with innate strength
Mustered from travail upon a weary land.
And yet, I catch a glimpse of your peace
That plays upon self-knowing features
Guided in the darkest night
To a future illuminated with splendor.

Your hands, strong and capable
Tell stories of woes
Where others fear to go.
Yet, you reach out into the bleakness
To conquer, lovingly,
Outrage and spiritual defeat.

The serenity of your spirit
Speaks to me
In the manner you tilt your head
And carry your body:
Your affection for others is complete
In the declarative manner you hold.

Your hands,
Though not delicate or daintily manicured,
Reveal caresses and hugs and
The love of a big heart.
Hands wide, enlarged by a firm clasp
In which sweetness
And your genuine kindness last.

I look at you and wonder
Whither I will go.
Shall I ever acquire
The wherewithal
To come to terms
With what you treasure so?

Shall I ever become sagacious
Ere my life is spent?
To follow where ancestors'
Footprints emblazoned a path?
To interpret the voices
Our intercessors have bestowed?
I look at you and wonder,
Will I ever know you?

# Stagecoach Mary

Don't know if you are aware
Of this one thing:
Way out West, gals
Were outnumbered—
Four men to each—
So they had choice pickins';
Some chose to marry,
Others did not.
But if a gal married
And he was rot,
She could divorce at daybreak
And remarry at dark.

Many a broken heart
Them guys did suffer
As gals knowingly and
With the upper hand
Took pleasure
In laying all sorts of traps
To lasso unsuspecting cattlemen.

Not every gal chose to play that game;
Some were too ornery
To be married to just one man.
And so the story goes
Of Mary Fields,
Our "Stagecoach Mary,"
Who chose never to let love kindle
Nor to marry.

Mary had a reputation:
The rough, tough, rowdy kind.

No man dared to cross her path,
Lest buckshot in his behind he'd find.
Mary drove a buck wagon,
And next to her on the slat,
Was her jug of whiskey
And her gun.
Her whiskey she loved better than anyone!

She used to haul supplies
For a mission in a Montana town.
They loved Stagecoach Mary;
'Til her notoriety was abound.
Off she'd go, a-suckin' on
A good cigar,
Then, when her duties were done,
She'd hang out at the bar.

She drank with the rowdiest of men
In from the range, and
The more they drank
The more their tempers did flame.
One day Mary got insulted
And challenged a man to a game:
No ordinary game—indeed,
"A duel," she called, "out in the street."

Lookin' mean and madder
Than a son of a gun,
Mary dug in her heels
As the man drew—
But his shot went awry.
Then Mary reared back
With careful aim,
And fired a shot

That sent him a-runnin',
Ne'er to be heard or seen again.

The men applauded at the bar
And rounds were drunk
Far into the night;
For all the gossip
Was about the gunslinger's fight.
But when the mission
Heard the news the next day,
The bishop fired Mary
For her gunslinging display.

Twas no problem for her,
As she puffed on her cigar.
Her renown, she knew,
Was as the toughest, roughest gal
Gunslinger in the West,
Who feared no man's hide.
Eventually, she saddled up,
Head driver on a stagecoach;
Esteemed in this new role
For she protected her cargo
With vim and vigor.

Many an outlaw grew disheartened
Once he encountered
Mary's wagon—or her figure.
Mary rode hard
Throughout the West
Feared by some—
Respected by the rest.
She chose to live her life
Without the distinction

Of being anyone's wife.
She'd rather be able
To come and go as she pleased.
Don't know of many men
Mary wouldn't fight
That dared to hinder her
From cigars and whiskey
Or staying out all night.

## Sortin' It Out

I need some teeth in this stuff,
Somethin' to cut the mustard
When the goin' gets rough.
Why, I reckon
My experience will have to do.
Can't do no reinventin'—
That don't feel true.

I'm gonna tell my story,
Gonna tell it as I am:
A cowhand
Who done run away
From the master's land.

Shucks, just wanna know
What it's like being free—
To feel the dusty wind sweep
Dirt clods in my face
As I roam hither and yon—
All over the place.

Wanna know what it means—
Sand betwixt my toes

As I escape to San Fran
By way of New Mexico.
I can only tell ya how it feels to me—
You gonna have to have
Your own vision to live—really free.

And I ain't gonna tell ya
What ya feel ain't so;
Shucks, I reckon paradise for me
Is in the journey
Of becoming free.

# SECTION TWO
## Workin' It—
## Cowboy Hustlin' and Rustlin'

# Sounds of a Cattle Run

Lickety-split,
Lickety-split,
Watchin' them dogs jump right o'er it.

Clickety-clack,
Clickety-clack,
Herdin' 'em into the pack.

Twiddle-dee-dum,
Twiddle-dee-dum,
Ain't much excitement on this cattle run.

Tumble-dum-dee,
Tumble-dum-dee,
They's tramplin' all o'er me.

Rickety-rack,
Rickety-rack,
Done broke my back tryin' to get 'em on track.

"May day!
May day!"
Mired in this blasted clay!

Drip, drip,
Drip, drip,
Epitaph reads, "This was his last trip."

Laid to rest
With the best:
Done made my way at last.

# Followin' the Wagon Trail

I cry: 'cause my fingers
Are numb with cold,
And my ankles are swelled again;
My legs, they swollen—so large
They look like tree limbs.

I cry: 'cause I don't know when
I'll see Mamma again.
She bade me go,
She stayed—"Too old."
Don't know when I'll see Mamma again.

I cry: tears swell to overflow,
And freeze upon my face.
I feel like I's ninety-nine years old;
Don't know if I'll make it
From this place.

I keep stumblin' o'er things
I cannot see on this rutted wagon trail,
Hands so crusted over with bleedin' and
Knees skint worsen than when
I fell a-chasin' brud' Jim.

Surely it's been three months or so
'Though it feels like years.
Done gone from blistering heat
To confounded cold
On this cursed Trail o' Tears.

Havin' to hide from peculiar folk,
Fearless and mean, is them.

Why they captured Stony and Elkee Mae,
And cousin Eliza too.
Heard tell they wup 'em.

Wup 'em good and
And make 'em work
Worse'n ole master do!
Guess we's the lucky ones—
Me and these other few.

See, we done hid in the bullrush
A fortnight or two
'Til those peculiar folk moved on—
A-draggin' our stuff,
And tramplin' our camp in two.

Can't help but cry,
As we trudge near stony craters
Wonderin' where this leads.
When am I gonna see Mamma again?
Is this trail gonna ever end?

I s'pose this musin'
Ain't gonna get me much …
But it's all I got 'til when
We get to the nor'west,
They say, that's where our journey ends.

Oh, Mamma, how I miss you!
How I wish we were at the end
Together in our village,
Reunited as a family,
Once again.

Maybe Mamma
I shouldn'a come,
Perhaps stayed with you;
Still can't quite understand
Why you made me to.

I don't know 'bout liberty;
All I know is you.
How I wish you be here
Or I be there wrappin'
My arms around you.

So, I keeps on cryin'—
Seems all I can do
While tryin' to keep up
In this gutted wagon rut –
Hopin' some point, Mamma,
I'll finally be with you.

## Connivin'

Connivin'—
It just don't guarantee survivin',
And it ain't that easy
For ev'ryone tryin'
To decide what to be.
You gotta ponder on the look,
Whether you want to be took
As demure on your dapple-gray mare,
Or brazen, trottin' round town
All devil-may-care.

And that's what I was
About a fortnight ago,

Comin' into town
For refreshment
And ... well, you know.
Now, I'm mighty fine, I think,
'Specially after I gulp
A couple o' drinks.
Sometimes I get to twirlin'
To and fro—
Sorta my way
O' lettin' folks know
I got some dough.
Seems sometimes it's all right
To strut about
Like you own the town—
But hon, let me tell you,
It ain't no fun
To be purty near shot down!

Like I was sayin' ...
A fortnight ago,
I came in from the range,
A-struttin' in my Stetson
And leather spurs,
Rifle at my side.
Swayin' hips,
Swiggin' gin,
And I got to hummin'
Some ole tune I think my mamma taught me
In the womb!
Went somethin' like—
"Ain't nobody bad enough
To take me down tonight;
Nobody—nobody—
Ain't even got an inklin'—

How to get me down in a twinklin'".

Now, there ain't no cause—
Y'all done gone off the beaten path—
Yeah, I see them looks
And I knows what y'all thinkin',
But I's talkin' 'bout arm-wrestlin'
Some of the best.
Many a night tryin' to warm our hides
In the cold starlight,
We'd challenge our comrades
To wrestle for a swig o' gin.

There I was propped 'gainst the table,
Hummin' my tune
Whilst scannin' the crowd
For some newcomer
To challenge me out loud.
I took another swig o' gin,
Wiped my lips,
And started my tune again—
When a fella quipped,
"Shut yo' face, for I know
I can put a whoopin' on ya
That'll send you home a-hurtin'."
I turned to see the offender
Standin' nearby commence to holler,
"What's the matter, gal, is you yeller?"
As I took another swig—
Nice and long and low—
I made a clearin' on the sideboard
For there's where I chose
To have my show.

Now, I admit there's some risk
When you commence to braggin',
But I was confident
I could nail this buffoon
And leave his tongue a-waggin'.
Ah! A quick twist of his wrist,
My arm was flat out on the wood!
Yet, not to be out done by such a tactic,
I tried again to break this fella;
And, again, he done like the other,
I was no match.
But I had no intention
Of springin' for his liquor.
That wasn't what I was about,
No siree—I was gonna make him
Serve me!

Well, you can imagine how it ended:
This fella was getting' sorta testy;
At some point, I guess he figured
I was a downright louse
Tryin' to shake him for a cowardly mouse.
The next thing I know,
I'm hurtlin' through the air,
Arms and feet flailin'
Like some wild mare.
I landed face down
In the water trough;
He jerked my head up
And grunted, "I reckon I should beat yo silly butt,
Exceptin' you's a gal—
And I'm tryin' mighty hard
To be respectin'.
I want you to remember me:

Big Jim—
Don't you never mess with him!
'Cause I got the angles, see.
Where I'm from, when you got the upper hand,
You done won.
So let this be a lesson to you, gal;
Next time you wanna take some fella
For a swig o' gin,
Make certain you ain't messin'
With ol' Big Jim.
I'll raise the stakes ev'ry time,
And I'll always whip yo' triflin' behind."

I guess you could say
My luck sorta ran out that night,
When this fella called me yella
And showed me up in da'fight.
It's been a while,
And you bet I took the lesson to heart.
That's why now all's I do
Is flutter and fan,
And switch and twitch,
Tryin' to snag some po' fools heart,
For a drink you say?
Sure, or whatever—
Ain't no shame;
Just know your game!
Connivin' don't guarantee survivin' ...
And remember
To equip yourself
With the look that's ripe
For baitin' the hook!

# Ridin' Herd

Oh, for the buoyant rivers wide
'Twixt Moon's Junction and Duty's Pride,
*Loomin' at the crossin'.*
Halted by the tempestuous ripples
Lappin' 'gainst boulder's edge.
Scannin' the prime place
To drive the longhorn breed,
Reckonin' with lively speed
Consequences of mishaps
Or ill-thought deeds—
*Loomin' at the crossin'.*

Slappin' cattle right and left,
Yelpin' orders to avert death,
While musterin' the command
Of the wind.
Plungin', shovin' cattle,
We go in
Like matadors,
Ushering our charges
Into this boisterous fate,
Castin' wide the gates of chance
With pompous air
And much circumstance—
*Loomin' at the crossin'.*

Through the tunnel of disguises
We masquerade our fears,
Bellowin' with deafened ears
And chargin' at breakneck pace
Through the river's portals.
Cattle intact, ready again

To commence the trail
Peaked with highs and lows.
Always hoverin'
As an ill-fated wind
Challenges us yet again
To explore ridin' herd
Through destiny's elusive door—
*Loomin' at the crossin'.*

## The Cattleman's Gift

Now as far as cattlemen are concerned,
There ain't no greater pleasure
Than drivin' herd through the plains,
Across mountainous terrains,
Or under thunderous cloud cover
Or through tumultuous waters.
For the spirit of the thing
Is in the journey, they claim.
So let it be packed to the brink
With sundry challenges,
Tied with the ribbons
Of nature's occurrences
And offered to the cattlemen—
Who unwrap this gift
Ceremoniously.

## Outlaws

Raided towns
Were the legacy we left you.
Rustled cattle,
Destroyed sheep herds too:
Meaner 'n a rattlesnake,

You always knew
When we came through.

Robbed trains,
Raided stagecoaches,
Burglarized homes
And businesses too;
They called us outlaws
'Cause you always knew
When we came through.

Raped women,
Assaulted men,
Murdered people too;
We were the meanest, baddest
Of all there was, and
You always knew
When we came through.

Hated by many,
Feared by some,
Revered by just a few;
Never mattered what you thought
We'd say or do.
'Twas our reputation far and wide:
Lived like hellions, died like vermin
Vengeful, furious and outrageous—
That was the legacy we left you.

## Transference

Adrenaline courses through my veins
While stallions stampede, thundering,
Majestic and regal in their flight, and

Breathtakingly beautiful is the sight.
How their glistening,
Powerful bodies absorb me,
Their moves orchestrated
With an arrogant flair;
Even their tails swish
Authoritatively through the air.

Nostrils aflame with vibrant breath,
Flared to challenge that end in death;
While defiant hooves
Stomp the ground
And threaten to trample
Anything that comes around.
Birds take flight at severe heights;
Hares, raccoons, and smallish creatures
That typically abound,
Disappear into foxholes with bated gasps
Until the ominous thunder releases its clasp.

Fixated by these creatures—free and wild,
Unimpeded by timidity or supposition—
My languishing spirit, refreshed
By the essence of these beasts,
Alights in power.
Suddenly, I stand taller—
More confident in my potential
As untarnished energy saturates me;
Anointed, finally able to express
Boundless spirituality and happiness.

# Carousing

I love those gamblin' halls,
Them glitterin' saloons and brothels
I frequent at the end of a trail run—
'Cause I be darned
If I ain't earned some fun!

Why, a thousand head of longhorns
Nearly stampeded me the other day,
As I was a-comin'
Down the Chisholm Trail
Toward Abilene!
I had to drive that herd
Through turbulent waters—
I'm sho' lucky I ain't drowned!

Them's the most peculiar
Herd o' cows;
They spook at the least ol' thing
Whether I'm just thinkin'
Of things to be mean
Beats me, but
Them cows are as temperamental
As a bride on her wedding night.

Though I ain't ever the lead
On a cattle drive
I deserve high times in the brothels
And gamblin' rows, that's for sure
'Cause it's a miracle I survive
My daily chores!

# Roaming the Range

The range is where I've been,
The range is where I roam,
Away from the perils
Of angry crowds at home;
Away from faces, bristling with hate
That despise the skin colors
Of God's children.

The range is where I've been,
The range is where I roam,
Free from ugly jeers
Of "nigger go home;"
Away from hatred
Embedded within generations
Of ignorance that haven't forgiven.

The range is where I've been,
The range is where I roam,
Free to dream and contemplate,
Standing proudly on my own;
Free to venture near or far
And lasso the reality
Of my dreams from above.

The range is where I've been,
The range is where I'll be,
Enraptured in the freedom
Of God's country.

# A Most Peculiar Sight

About six weeks ago
When I was travellin'
About the plain,
I ran across a feller
Who appeared to be crawlin'
On the terrain.
So, I pulled up beside him
On my dapple-gray
And said, "Howdy, partner;
Why you in this way?"

Then he commenced to tell me
A tale I'd often heard:
How he lost his way
Drivin' a cattle herd.
Said he was somewhere
'Twixt Dundee's Crossing
And Shenandoah,
When some huge, cruel creature
Bowled him o'er.

"I did not see it comin';
'Twas like a furry ball,
But it knocked me for a loop," says he,
"Cattle, herd and all."
"My pinto collapsed beneath me,"
The feller continued on,
"I fell into a hollow place
Where no creature should e'er be born.

"It was the damndest thing;
That place where I just fell—

It was kinda like being suspended
Right 'twixt heaven and hell.
The sun was glarin' high,
But 'neath me was a bush
Fastened tight with prickles galore
To my very tush."

"And you can figure
The more I twisted and turned,
Them stickers pierced me mightily,
Just like a brandin' iron.
So squirming didn't do no good;    .
My butt was stingin' mighty hot
Like I'd been hit point-blank right there
With a load of buckshot."

Now the damnedest thing of all
(That left me much perplexed)
Is how this feller got loosed
From his dire net?
So I say to the feller,
"How is it your hide,
Ain't fastened to nuthin' now—
That I can plainly see—
Well, how is it you managed
To get yo'self all free?"

The feller commenced to grinnin'
And asked me for a smoke.
He stroked his beard a while,
Then he rolled his tobacco.
Once he smoothed the paper,
Got it nice and thin,
He took a puff, and then

Began his tale again.
"Well now," says the feller,
"I'd been drivin' hard and long
And as you know, with cattle,
Them things can go off wrong.

"Now most of 'em, when I got lost,
High-tailed it lickety-split—
'Ceptin' one ole critter,
Who didn't have a wit.
He commenced a-gnawin' and a-pokin'
Right up on my backside.
He was mighty amused with his proddin',
And after a while, my pants began to slide.

"Somehow I wiggled out—
But not without several more
Of those prickles, damned things,
Piercing me in my rear."
Then the feller stood up,
And I could plainly see
His mangled trousers dangled
Loosely around his knees.
And when he turned
To strike a match against the rock,
I beheld his very scarred
And bloodied buttocks.

"Gosh darn," says I to the feller
Who straightened up his back.
"Won't you take my jacket?"
I pulled it from my knapsack,
And I tossed it to the feller.
"Mighty obliged," says he.

"Now if you can lend me a ride,
I'd like to get to Dundee."
And so, I hoisted the feller at my side.
A mighty sight made we.

After several hours, into town
We moseyed, he and me.
Folks was starin', gawpin',
Like I done swiped a canary.
And when I asked
What the starin' was about,
A horse rider whispered,
"You got Jesse in your clout."
Now Jesse was a thief,
Wild and free, known for his intrigue.
A gentler feller one couldn't find,
But I wasn't in his league.

"Is that rightly so?" I asked the feller,
With the scarred buttocks.
"Yeah," says he—"Some kinda hero—
Wid my butt hanging free; just my lot."
So that's the tale of this feller
I met out on the plain,
His butt was naked,
Travelin' the dusty terrain,
Still, I'd do it all again;
I know his heart was carefree,
I'd help him even if he is a thief,
Tryin' to make it to Dundee.

# A Special Breed

And when we contemplate the ways
Of cowhands:
Some ostentatious,
Some jolly, others not.
You gotta keep it all in perspective
'Cause that is their lot.

When you exposed to all weather—
Cloudy, rainy, or freezin' cold—
You can bet your gray whiskers
This can make a feller seem old:
Old afore his time,
Old afore his prime,
Old afore he meets his mate,
Or old afore he even dates.

On the other hand, some venture to say,
'Tis the luck o' the draw
When you live this way,
And it has some advantages too:
You get to be perceived as old and wise,
Which (as you know) ain't true.

But better to be thought of in kindly ways
For the duration of a cowhand's days:
Like a feller nursin' a broken heart,
Or a feller who's as carefree as a lark,
Or a feller who journeys with the gods,
Or plays with angels in their yards.

All I'm offerin' is some explanation
For the diversity that's found
In the cowboy population!

# Speculation From the Shadows

There I was in the shadows
At ole Pritchett's bar again;
When in walked Big Sam,
Lookin' meaner'n a
Brahma bull
And madder'n a red hen.
He sauntered to the back, along the wall
Proppin' one dusty boot up
On the rickety stool there.

He was leanin',
Kinda ponderin' havoc, I 'spect,
Nonetheless, I was determined
To give him no disrespect.
Why, I heard tell yesterday
Casey done throwed all Big Sam's belongings
In the street—
Somethin' 'bout pay up or else
Find another place to sleep.
For Big Sam had the reputation
For spendin' all his wages
At Lucinda's gamblin' hall
A ways down the street,
Or over the corner
Where Ray Moore and his boys usually meet.

There he was, lookin' spiteful and ornery—
I wasn't 'bout to step in his way—
Why, that fella may blow me clean away!
Ya know, Big Sam shoots buffalo,
And when the season's at its end,
He goes huntin' slimy snakes and cougar skins.

51

He'd slice 'em up, yessiree,
And eats 'em off the blade of his Bowie knife.

Sometimes seasoned with red pepper
And a side dish of brown beans,
And when he felt they's seasoned best,
He splits 'em open
And puts 'em to the test.
If'n they smelled like a steer's liver
Turned inside out,
Big Sam swallows 'em down
With pickled pig snout.

Personally, I think Big Sam eats 'em raw
For sheer devilry.
Why, can't ya imagine
The guts of a man
Who eats raw snake
And cougar?
His innards must be in knots
Tryin' to digest such a meal …
But to Big Sam,
It just wasn't any big deal.

So I watched him
From the shadows of the bar;
Like I said, I wasn't gonna go too far
Gettin' in the face of a man
Whose smile was twisted in pain,
Like the grimace
Of some wayward soul
Who'd been declared insane.
There he was a-ponderin'
What next to do,

No place to go,
And his rent past due.

Now, I tell ya,
I think one's pretty brave
To challenge a raw-cougar-eatin'
And snake-lovin' ex-slave-cowboy
On the fly.
Foolhardy, how's I describe such stupidity.
Anyhow, you can imagine
The ruckus that it would muster
Notifyin' him he's gotta pay up or else;
Heck, I would've donated him the place
Rather than encounter the grimace
On that hateful face.

But cowardly ain't the way some folk be,
Only wizened souls like little ol' me;
Souls that value livin' another day
Would let Big Sam go on his way;
Souls like me, who recognize that some things
Ain't that much of a crime.
His rent is past due—so what?
At least life's freely flowin' today;
Heck, let 'im just have his way!
I don't know—is it egos in the end
That cause such disaster
That clearly shouldn'ta been?

Anyhow, the pipsqueak
Who tried to stare Big Sam down
Ain't been seen nowhere in town.
I hear tell Big Sam has run of the place;
Aint nobody gonna check it out, that's for sure.

'Cause most folk who value life,
Would rather not knock on Big Sam's door.

## The Shootout at Dawn

Now this ain't no tale 'bout duelin' folk
Or a lover's quarrel.
This here's the tale of a deal gone stale
'Cause a fella got to disbelievin'.

I had just finished up my chores
When Jerry asked me
To accompany him down to the store,
A good mile or two away—
And as I had done a good day's work
I felt like quenchin' my thirst
Wid a cold cola or ale—
Whichever came first.

So, we strutted on into town
Laughin' with each other
And just plain clownin' around.
When we happened upon a fella
Carryin' a stick,
A-twistin' and a-turnin'
It this way and that—
Actin' like he had the tail
Of a runaway bull.

Suddenly he bolted
Like somethin' had set him aflame
Whilst he was a playin'
This twistin' and a-turnin' game.

I says to Jerry, "What you make of that?
There goes a fella behavin' like
A dude who lost his hat."
Jerry peers over the top
Of his rims at me,
Tilts his brim, and then, says he,
"That fella is a metal hunter
For a special find—
So he can leave ranchin'
And cowdoggin' behind.

Ain't you ne'er heard of that?
Why, 'em metal detectors
Could help you land some gold,
Or at the very least,
Perhaps a rare coin or two.
And, once you get that,
Your cowdoggin' days is through."

"Hmmm," says I,
As we rounded the bend,
"I reckon we oughta get ourselves one.
Ain't no sense lettin' one fella
Have all the luck;
There oughta be a way
We can earn a buck."

Jerry slipped his brim
Further back on his head,
And peered o'er his shoulder
Like he was afraid
He'd be whipped from behind.
"Shucks, let's jest ask him
If we can borrow it," says he.

"Wouldn't need but an hour or two.
I got a hankerin' for a place
We can go on our own hunt—
And probably find a bunch."

"Hmmm," says I,
"Reckon he'd lend that contraption
For a time or two?"
"I s'pose he will, if'n we pay him for the trouble
We put him through."

So we approached the stranger
And Jerry commenced to askin'
If he'd lend to us the contraption
For a sixpence.
The dude agreed,
And we promised to be back by three;
We'd meet up at the store
'Twixt Franklin and Calvary.

Soon as the fella got outta sight,
Jerry and I crept up a nearby ledge
In the direction of a hideout
Where thieves once abode;
Jerry's was sure that there
We'd find a remnant of their load.

Jerry commenced to workin' that thing;
I was the lookout,
Makin' sure ain't nobody watchin'
As we made our search for treasure
That would yield
Bounty beyond measure.

You can figger, eventually,
We hit upon a coin or two—
No doubt fallen from the robbers' stash
In their haste
To divvy up their bounty
And escape the place.
We then headed on back
To our rendevous point,
To give the fella his contraption
And to get outta that joint.

There was the fella
Leanin' against the wall,
Piece of straw stuck betwixt his teeth,
Legs crossed, arms folded,
Eyeing me, and Jerry.
"You fellas have any luck prospectin'?
Where'd ya go?
What ya see?
Y'all been out there 'til almost three."

Now I don't know the code for such,
But I didn't think blabbin' bout
What ya found was in the rules,
So I thought the best thing
Was to play this real cool.

I says to the fella,
"What d'ya think?
Why, that stick a yours is just a big fink!
Ain't nothin' to this prospectin'
That I can see, but a sore back
From bendin' and pickin' up metal bits

Just to see if our luck was a-turnin'
At any time afore three."

Jerry sorta swayed
From his right foot to his left,
And nodded his agreement
Wid a tilt of his hat.
And that's how it ended, just like that—

'Til around quarter to five
The next mornin',
When we woke to some rustlin'.
I glimpsed a shadowy figure
And reached for my shooter;
I was about to make my mark
At whatever was after us.

But afore I could make out
What was what,
I heard our gunnysack
Crash to the floor.
I shot one round into the air,
Then another and another,
To let the intruder know I had 'im.
And Jerry reared up from his bunk
And threw his boot
At the shadow near his trunk.

Next thing happened—
Well, I ain't quite clear
'Bout the sequence,
But somethin' went
A-yelpin' into the dark.
I jumped to my feet

To see it's hind side disappear,
And noted it was the fella
With the contraption.
Clearly, now I sure knowed
What he intended—

He was attemptin'
To haul off our booty!
But as he rounded the corner,
The drawstring slipped;
Coins went spillin' and rollin' away.
But he was in such a hurry
To get out of there quick,
He took no notice of losin' it!

By this time, a coupla folks
Had gathered to see
What was happenin'
To cause such a ruckus.
As we sauntered toward the door
Jerry glanced at his backside;
He noted a piece of cloth was missin'
From a prominent place on his hide.

He just grinned and, placing his hand
Over the bare spot,
A twinkle in his eye,
Says he, "Y'all missed the best part!

"For a shootout occurred
On the lawn at dawn
'Twixt two burly folk
Who hated each other
And plotted to do in one another.

They trailed off into the woods—
That's all we sure know."

Now, I know y'all is
Smart enough to figger,
But in case you ain't,
I'll make it plain.
Tellin' this tale
Was to distract anyone
Who might be tempted
To snoop through our stuff for our loot.
'Sides, y'all know that kind of doin'
Can leave you limpin'
Once we commence to givin' you the boot.

## The Track

A-travelin' from the Mason-Dixon line
Several months ago,
I came upon a situation
Where trouble seemed to flow.
I was a gazin' out the glass
Of the Lexington train
When my eyes rested upon a feller
Screechin' out in pain.
I reared up and yanked the pulley
Two or three times, it seemed,
'Til the steward came up to me
To see what was my need.

I pointed to the feller
Over yonder way,
Who appeared to be tortured
'Cause of some trouble there that day.

The steward immediately called
Some assistance down the line.
Well, naturally the train
Did not stop to find,
And I just hope and pray
Someone came to rescue
That feller from his agony.

Eventually, I lay back
And closed my eyes in sleep,
Soon lost to another world
Where fantasy was for keeps.
By the time I awakened
It was time to disembark,
And while I started down the steps,
That feller bade me hark.
He was only in my mind, but
Still it threw me off.
I wasn't sure just what to do,
So ignored it with a scoff.

Well, I collected my belongings
And bid passers-by *adieu*
And went about my business—
Going to visit my nephew.
He was a burly fella now,
Done grown a heap since last I been
In this part of the country
Seein' and visitin' kin.
We hugged and slapped each other
Mightily on the back,
And I climbed into his wagon
Headed south along the track.

It was a starry night and moonlit;
My heart, overwhelmed with love,
Reached to heaven for tranquility,
Which descended like a dove.
Well, there I was,
Inhalin' calmness, one might say—
The beauty of the evening
When my thoughts of the day
Returned me to the feller
I saw in agony along the way.
Though, come to ponder,
Ain't that how it always is?
All the highs and the lows
With the mid-ground like an abyss?
You become a memory of another
(Of whom you ain't even aware)
Who sees you in your agony,
Perplexed and in despair.
I reckon these moments spent
Gazin' at other passers-by,
Serve as our reminder
Of how time flies.

So take the time to
Gaze into the night,
Inhale the beauty of stars
Twinkling and shining bright.
And remember,
Before your time comes
To cross the other track
Live and do the best you can,
'Cause there is no turnin' back!

# The Bronco Rider

My story's simple.
Only I can tell
How I survived the demons
Of a cowboy's hell.

I was a master bronc rider, you see;
I lassoed the devil in his cell;
I saw death a-comin' and challenged her,
For I was the bronc rider from hell.

Done my livin' the way I chose to,
Fearless, toughened from many a fight.
Nobody dared tell me what to do or not,
Ain't nothin' sacred in my sight.

One day brings out this runt
Determined to bust me up as a test.
He challenged me to rider's duel
To take my place as the best.

What did he ask? You'll never believe:
To lasso a long-horn steer,
But not the usual way, no sir—
With one hand tied behind my ear!

Now many a cowpoke would say
Didn't matter reputation was at stake:
"Man, you crazy! Ain't no way down!"
But I'd show this fool what it takes!

Would this be the end for me?
We settled upon a time and place;

Many were gathered, wagers galore,
Betting to see my disgrace.

The crowd applauded the stranger,
As he smoothly lassoed the steer,
And I cannot lie—he did it fast
With one hand behind his ear!

Astride my mustang I sat tall.
Tense was the crowd, their yelps strong;
Many were in doubt I could eke it out,
That I would carry this test along.

My horse pranced around a bit,
Tossing his head from side to side,
Clenching his teeth and whinnying loud
In fearless, trusting pride.

Calmly I dashed alongside
And looked the steer in the eye.
Suddenly I leaped from my horse to his back
And whispered aloud, "You's mine."

I clenched my teeth into its upper lip,
And fastened my grip about his neck,
Forcing him to his knees and onto his side—
"I got him," proclaimed I with pride.

Signaling my mustang who came near
As the crowd all wildly cheered,
He quickly drew up and lowered himself
For me to mount from the rear.

While the crowds roared with laughter
I looked around and saw my challenger agape.
Dazed by the stunt, all he could manage was a grunt,
Like a dumbfounded stupid ape.

For I had done more than he, you see:
Not only wrestled the steer to the ground
But with one hand fastened behind my ear
I bit the steer's lip until he lay sound!

No one's ever been able to take my place;
I hold it out with pride,
For my notoriety from this challenge
Traveled far and wide:

As the bronc rider from hell

That a steer with his teeth he did fell!

# SECTION THREE
## Romancin'—
## Cowboy Love Stories

# The Romance of Cowboy Jim and Marilyn

Don't know if you ever heard told
One of the most fanciful romances of old …
In the chance you weren't around then,
Let me tell you 'bout Marilyn and Cowboy Jim.

Marilyn was one of the rancher's daughters—
He had seven of 'em, you see—
And each of them was as handy with a herd
And a gun as you or me.

Rancher Jack was proud of his gals;
Why, they could cut cattle outta a herd
As smooth as churning butter,
Singin' sweetly as a bird.

And when it came to conjuring up
Chow out on the trail,
They were mighty creative with chuck-wagon pots—
Lawdy, what a delicious smell!

We'd have jackrabbit and antelope stew,
And prairie chicken shot with Marilyn's gun.
Yep, them gals could cook up a slop and shoot a six
As good as Rancher Jack and his sons!

One day, while driving the herd over the prairie,
Spotted an outlaw on the horizon
Headed our way, as best we could see, so
We took our places, and prepared that six-gun.

Discreet behind rock and thickets
Plotting an attack to feature Marilyn—

As only a pretty gal can, you see,
Marilyn was to create a distraction.

We hid behind trees, waitin' for the varmint,
And right when we got to the marked spot,
With a calculated tilt of her Stetson,
Marilyn came out on her horse at a trot

So that her braids fell loose—
Indeed, 'twas no mistakin' it—
Marilyn wasn't no cowboy, no sir!
And the varmint could see she'd been fakin' it.

She fidgeted with her split skirt
As she let her left hand slide
Along the mule ears of her scalloped boots
And the spurs on her cowhide.

'Twas a strange thing, what next happened:
For we seen the outlaw stop abruptly in his tracks
And gaze upon Marilyn's coarse brown hair
Flappin' in waves all down her back.

His pause was just enough,
'Cause as Marilyn crept on closer
We swung the rope o'er his head
And pulled the knot to a choker.

Oddly, he did not struggle,
Just appeared transfixed
By the image of Marilyn
Astride her sweet horse, Candlestick.

When he spoke, he merely asked
Was that an image he was beholdin'
For ne'er had he seen such a pretty lass
In all his days a-wanderin'!

Ole Cowboy Jim happened up the trail about then,
All enthralled by Marilyn's beauty.
He couldn't help but be entranced—
And he'd surely do his duty.

And when he saw the outlaw's stupor
He galloped up from the rear
And pulled his pistol and fired a shot
That nicked the outlaw's ear.

Marilyn, indeed impressed
With such chivalry and boldness,
Looked dreamy-eyed at Cowboy Jim
And pulled the reins on the harness.

Jim quickly trotted 'longside her
And gallantly encircled her waist;
With one swoop of his strong arms
On his horse the gal he did place.

Why, Marilyn held on to him tight
As the horse began to dash;
Like a bee clinging to the honey,
She went with him like a flash.

'Bout a couple of years ago,
I heard someone tell the story
That Marilyn and Cowboy Jim
Actually did marry.

On the eve of the escapade,
Further up the trail,
They detoured in Montana
At a resort hotel.

It so happened that in that place
They found a man of the cloth
Who saw them besotted one with another
And tied the knot for the newly betrothed.

So, my friend, if you happen along a drive
And find outlaws a-plottin'
You never know what the future holds
For those with whom you be trottin'.

Some encounters end with gun battle,
A few end with a treaty,
But nary a one I know'd 'til this
Ended with matrimony.

The attack might come from Cupid—
You just will never know when—
Like it did for Cowboy Jim
And pretty Marilyn!

## An Expectant Cowgal's Introduction

I started to wear a burlap sack
'Cause I no longer fit in my cowgal chaps.
As you can see, I'm bigger'n most,
But of this one thing I'm inclined to boast:
I can still see my feet, long, slender and trim;
Why, I'm the latest version

Of southwestern pregnant women!

Givin' birth in these parts ain't much to bolt
From deliverin' a calf or a colt:
Just hitch my feet to the chuck-wagon wheels
And tell me when to push instead of when to squeal,
And then, as sure as I'm a cowgirl,
I'll introduce to the world
A squallin' child named Jamie Lynn Pearl!

## Isom Dart

Let me tell you the story
Of ol' Isom Dart,
How he broke my will and my soul,
And also my heart.
He was as elusive as them horses
He was always chasin';
You think you landed him,
Then you find—time, it was a wastin'.

I ain't proud to say it,
But wit' Isom Dart
My lovin' was in trouble
From the very start.
He was as slippery
As a big river fish.
I ne'er was quite sure
If I was his only dish.

He'd say things
That got me wonderin' in that way:
Has he been a-rollin'
With another in the hay?

And, although he assured me
I's his only hon,
Sometimes I hear him
Call the name of another one.

Now, I ain't really complainin'—
I guess it's as it should be,
When tryin' to lasso a twitchy heart
Like that of unconquerable Isom Dart.
His unquenchable spirit
Was meant to be free
To rove across the plains
Of all humanity.

Ah, but how striking,
How strong and proud is that man!
I found his sensibilities
Too hard to withstand.
And so, I am as helpless
As a calf not up on its feet,
When it comes to lovin' Isom Dart—
Who insists on being free.

So colorful, so dashing,
Always a tale to be told:
How often he got holed up
With thieves on the road
For my lover was a rustler,
A varmint, plain to see:
The best of 'em, of course,
Was what others have told me.

Truth is, he was good
At whatever he put his mind to:

Did bronc-bustin' from the Rio Grande
All up to Colorado.
A talented horseman was Dart—
Swift, skilled, and deft
With both his hands and both his feet,
As good with right as left.

Alas, he tried to abide by the law
But the tale of some daring feat
Would have Isom at risk
To meet the challenge or be beat.
He had to win at horse rustlin'—
No matter the draw or prize.
I wish it hadn'ta been so,
But I saw it with my own eyes.

Isom got caught up
In an ambush one day,
All the gang was killed—
But Isom managed to get away.
'Twas enough for him to re-think,
Reform himself and get clean;
And so he set himself
On a different path to freedom.

He angered many a cattleman
For his contrite ways—
So much so that he was forced
To hide out most of his days.
And that's when I'd go to him;
He'd get the word out to me
Through one of his old pals or pokes
To meet clandestinely.

I lived for those times
When I'd be with my lover,
So dashing, daring, and refined;
I'd never have blown his cover.
We'd steal away in secret,
And lovin' him was heaven divine.
Hungrily making spirited love,
Thinkin' it may be our last time.

And then it happened.
I heard it told—the finale that I feared:
My beloved Isom Dart was shot and killed
By one whose path he'd cleared.
An unforgiving hunter who refused
To believe Isom's reform,
That he was makin' an honest livin'
And not stealing off the horn.

So here I'm left to tell
The end of the sad, sad tale
Of my beloved Isom:
How he wandered freely the trail
And lived a life of splendor,
Most adventurous to see,
For his insatiable spirit
Insisted on being free.

And some would judge me—yet I have no shame
How I loved a man many disdained.
When I realized this horse rustler's heart
Would never be mine from the start,
I accepted the best and the worse of it
Lovin' Isom Dart—
A man of indomitable passion
And a twitchy heart.

# Mopin' John

Mopin' John was a cowhand
At ole Bell Prickett's ranch
Who did his chores and duties
Without pomp or circumstance.
Regarded as mediocre in most things,
He had a peculiar habit that revealed
Another side to his character
Which was amusin' to some:
Mopin' John, you see,
Had a deep hankerin'
For dancin' and boozin'
Wid mean women.

Now, 'tis true weren't many gals
Around in those parts,
But Mopin' John, it seems,
Was a master of the courtin' arts.
Maybe it was his talent,
Or maybe it was his list—
'Cause the gals he selected
Were meaner'n a snake's hiss.
'Most every Saturday evening
When his chores were done,
Away to the dance hall he would run.
Many a ranch hand laughed to watch:
Hat in hand and a hunch in his back,
Mopin' John would venture
Near 'em tough gals
Like a scairt pussycat.

Amused by his style,
Some would scoff, most would joke,

But because his demeanor was sincere,
Many took up with that cowpoke.
And then he would stand like a bronc-rider
Who won the prize at a bullfight,
And away he would dance with his gal
Off into the night.
Round and round on the dance floor,
They would twirl a doe-see-doe,
A two-step, a turkey trot—
Any dance was a go!

Many a boot heel
He'd wear down in this fashion:
For dancin' with the meanest gals
Was Mopin' John's passion!
Lots of folk would travel—
They'd come from near and far—
Just to watch Mopin' John
Perform like some star.
Oblivious to gapes and wisecracks
Like a man crazed in a trance,
Rattled by nothin' was Mopin John
'Cept'n when the music stopped the dance.

Then Mopin' John would wet his whistle
With a long, cold drink from the bar,
And after fetching his partner,
Off he'd go back to the floor.
His gal was usually caught up
In some corner brawl,
But once he got her sorted,
Away the two would twirl.
Watchin' Mopin' John dance,
You could see his obvious delight

At workin' up a good, clean sweat
Long into the night.

One evenin' I remember,
A stranger came into town
And stood in the back of the saloon,
Head tilted slightly down—
But fascinated was he,
His eyes fixed open wide
On the gal who was a-swingin'
At Mopin' John's side.
After some time,
The man approached the pair
And beckoned the gal for a dance
As Mopin' John stood there.
Why, that gal just glared at him
Like he was hot cow dung
And spewed a string of epithets
As his face dropped and hung.

Slowly he turned on his heel
And sauntered off, all slack—
But that gal, why, she followed him
And then tapped him on his back.
He turned, and wouldn't you know,
She belted him square in the jaw!
The stranger collapsed in a heap
The quickest you ever saw.
Meanwhile, Mopin' John
Just quietly stood aside,
And as he watched his gal,
His chest swelled in pride;
She defended her right to dance
With the cowhand who had a passion

For the toughest, strongest cowgals—
A-twirlin' them in timely fashion.

They may have been the meanest gals
That ever dwelled in the West;
But Mopin' John was the feller
These gals loved the best!

## The Saga of Loulee-Mae Earl

What can I tell ya about this gal,
The sassiest you'll ever see?
She was as brazen as the cowpoke's son
Who roamed the ranch of Johnnie Lee.
She ne'er bit her tongue 'bout nothin',
Determined to have the last word;
Yes sir, Loulee-Mae made sure
She was gonna be heard.

Oh, there was an occasion,
You can be sure,
Where shuttin' her trap
Would-a been better for her.
It happened back a while ago,
On Johnnie Lee's ranch, The Corale.
A couple ole' pokes was spinnin'
All kinds of yarns and tales.

Then they took bets on who could rope most tight.
Well, the knots being tied were fancy indeed:
Like the Butterfly, and Double-Splayed Loop,
Even the Triple Crown and the Bowline on a Bight;
Them boys knew their stuff;
It was gonna be hard to choose

Which one was gonna be dubbed the best,
And which one was gonna lose.

'Round 'bout the time the bettin's nearly done
And the funnin' well underway,
Down the pathway a-piece comes Loulee-Mae.
Ready to have her say.
"Aw, them tricks aint nothin'—
Jus' the boring same ole thing …
Why I'll betcha neither one of y'all
Can tie a Double O Ring."

The fellas looked at one another,
Realizin' this was somethin' new,
Sizin' up the moment—
Was a gal gonna be the one to outdo?
"Why Loulee-Mae," said one,
"A Double O Ring, for real?
You know that knot is tricky,
Less'n you got the feel."

"I'll betcha," added the other,
"You ain't never tied a one—
Ain't tied no Double O Ring
To a plank hangin' in the sun."
With that, he pointed to the plank
Outside the barn, up high,
And exchanged a glance of doubt
With the other guy.

"Aw, heck!" exclaimed Loulee-Mae,
"A Double O Ring tied yonder?
That's somethin' I can do any ole day,
Don't you even wonder."

The fellas and Loulee-Mae
Made towards the barn,
While wagers on whether she could do it
Were pilin' high 'til bettin' was done.

Loulee-Mae took a step or two
Slightly angled from the barn,
And, like a lasso in her hand,
She whipped the rope like yarn.
But unbeknownst to her
As she hurled it towards the plank,
She realized only too late
Her boot heel caught the shank!

Up she went a-whirlin'
Like a calf caught in a lasso;
Topsy-turvy, she swayed,
Her boot lashed to the plank just so.
Helplessly she squealed,
Just like a pig in a poke—
A hilarious sight to be sure,
To be a butt end of a joke.

They stared up at Loulee-Mae,
Peals of laughter shakin' the crowd:
Wipin' eyes and holdin' bellies,
Some fell to the ground.
With furious fists, she beat the air,
Her petticoats high overhead
And bloomers all a-rufflin',
Like feathers on a goose bed.

So, for once, I have to admit,
And in an unusual way,

Loulee-Mae, like usual,
Had the last word that day.
Come to think of it,
It's what cemented her reputation
Of having the last word—
No matter the trepidation.

But there was also a lesson
Loulee-Mae learned that day
Whether she'll ever follow it
Or do nothin' but play:
Ne'er wager on what you
Don't know you can do—
'Cause them kinda wagers
Have a way of hauntin' you!

## A Cowboy's Love Song

I'm off to the highlands,
The highlands, the highlands;
I'm off to the highlands, my love.
For there I left my maiden,
My maiden, my maiden;
For there I left my maiden, my love.

And when I get there,
I get there, I get there,
And, when I get there, my love,
I'll ask her to marry,
To marry, to marry;
I'll ask her to marry, my love.

We'll go o'er yonder,
O'er yonder, o'er yonder;

We'll go o'er yonder, my love,
Where we'll live in the sunset
The sunset, the sunset;
We'll live in the sunset, my love.

Too long have I tarried,
I tarried, I tarried;
Too long have I tarried, my love.
So there I will marry,
Will marry, will marry;
I will marry my maiden—my love.

## The Horse Rustler

Lord a'mighty,
He was awful good-lookin'
Eyes bright, big, and brown;
I don't care what they called him:
He was the most good-lookinest
Man in town!

His voice was smooth,
Made for sweet-talkin'
More than anyone's could be;
His skin black as night
Shone in the starlight.
I'd give him anything, even me.

Beyond horses in the corral
Or under the tree,
I'd hear him a-talkin' in the woods.
It took all I could do
To hold myself back
From givin' him my goods.

What a smile he did grin
Wide, And flashed at me
From ear to ear.
Why, didn't he know,
He could have whatever he wanted—
I wouldn't disappear!

Yep! I was easy—as easy as can be:
Why, I'd proclaim to be a hussy,
If he'd only look at me.
Many days and nights I lay dreamin'
'Bout him a-rescuin' me
From the monotony of cattle ranchery.

*Steal me away,*
*Oh great lover;*
*Take me away, briskly.*
*Let us dash over the horizon*
*And off to another land*
*Where we'll live forever, peacefully.*

How I dared dream about him,
His hands beneath my knees,
Laying me gently upon the ground;
I would watch his big, black hands
Needing little guidance from me
Caressing me all around.

Ah! Let him take me
Freely as he would
The horses he stole away!
Awaken me not; let the fantasy abide

For I am hopelessly in love
With a horse thief, rough as the day!

Beckon I from afar,
Telling him he's welcome
To come closer to my breasts;
Look deeply into my eyes,
Feel my passion for thee,
And there you will find rest.

*I've watched you talk many a horse*
*Away from his caring master*
*In a sweet, natural style;*
*Surely, you can speak to me too,*
*And my passion, imprisoned within,*
*In like tones beguile.*

Alas! Dear gal, a horse thief
Is enraptured by the chase.
After the capture, the thrill does cease!
Relinquish him to frivolous barmaids;
His heart for you will ne'er be,
So catch him—and then release!

# Free Spirit

Have you e'er heard the tale
Of Carlita Lee,
Reared by a half-Injun, half-Creole
And a mammy as black as the night sky,
With eyes as bright as shining stars
Lightin' up the earth?
Carlita was as beautiful as she was funny
And generous in spirit as she wanted to be;

However, she had this dang affinity
For other wives' husbands no matter the enmity.

Carlita was assuredly blessed
With all the world's graces
And the ageless amenities
Men have been beholden too.
Indeed, she was envied by gals
As much as she was revered by men.
Carlita was the talk for miles around—
Of her exploits, there seemed no end.

A fortnight ago, I heard tell
That Carlita nearly lost it all.
Good looks, dough, and a stream of men
Who kept Carlita in the style she'd
Grown accustomed to:
Flashy, sassy, and certainly bold,
You mightn' have a hard time believin'
How this tale unfolds.
Yessir; Carlita's name
Drooled from nearly ev'ry man's lips—
As they either gazed or daydreamed
'Bout her voluptuous curves …
Well I can see you get my gist:
It was said Carlita was God's answer
To man's happiness.

Anyhow, as the story goes,
Carlita was out on her usual stroll,
Whereupon she was befallen
To a couple of men—
Who were determined
To take Carlita home with 'em.

Now this she didn't mind—that's for sure,
'Cause Carlita gone home many times before
With the lonesome, the weary,
And the creative too;
Why, that Carlita was a friend
To many—perhaps too many.
But it seems these two rascals
Had some devious plan
To take Carlita
And ensure she'd never be seen
Again.

They'd a hankerin' to have her
All to themselves—not to be shared.
Shucks, you guessed it:
That wouldn't work,
'Cause Carlita, generous as she can be,
Was a spirited thing
And insisted she always remain free.
So these fools, they took a gunnysack,
Swooped Carlita up,
And carried her on their backs.
She was kickin', screamin', and hollerin'
Like a heifer surrendin' to birth;
I swear, I ain't never heard more gasps
And expletives than she spouted:
Clearly, Carlita was desperate to be ousted.

Now Carlita was the salt of purty near
Ev'ry man's earth,
So when word got out Carlita had disappeared
Off the dusty streets of Abilene, well,
You can't imagine the pitiful scene.
Men were moanin' like they

Done lost their best longhorn!
Finally, at the O-shay Bar
Near the end of Cutler Street,
Several of the men, not willin' to accept defeat
Came up with a plan to search high and low
To find their lassie—no matter the cost;
For convinced were they that she was lost.

'Course, you can betcha,
Their women weren't about to search;
They done figured Carlita
Was in a predicament
They reckoned she caused in her way;
It suited 'em mighty fine that
Carlita wasn't around that day.

Seems though, one of the fellers
Got wind of the kidnappin' that occurred,
'Cause one of the rascals
That'd been involved in the connivin'
Had swaggered over to the O-shay Bar
And commenced a-braggin'.
Why, he was so puffed up
'Bout his escapade
He nearly fell over in his drink,
As he boasted 'bout
The best lovin' he ever had,
And was sure to keep gettin'—
For he had a bonny mare, high-steppin for sure,
But he was bound to tame her!
He brooked no defeat, sure
She'd bend in the heat of his scorn
That he'd apply at dawn.

"Why, shucks," said he,
"She's the purtiest thang this side of the West!"
And that means beyond Abilene,
For women there were noted for being mean.
Feller added, "She's sweeter'n
Honey to a fly, and mo' tender
Than the best steak I done ever ate,
With a smile so purdy,
She sure 'nuf makes it hard to hate.
And once nestled with this lass," he declared,
"All the chaos of the day
Just melted in a heap
Like a bale of burnin' hay."

Now he kept on—
This fool braggart, and it wasn't hard to see
That he spoke of none other than Carlita Lee.
They learnt of the plot
And they learnt a-plenty more …
So they moved aside to another place
To commence to schemin'
How they could rescue Carlita
From this disgrace.
The braggart's loose lips told it all:
Where Carlita was hid
Yonder way at the deserted bungalow
Down by the bales near Critters Cheek,
Several miles outside of Abilene.
So they mused
They'd just keep a' pourin' the gin and ale
And soon this fool would be of no avail.
Indeed, he finally tuckered out—
Snortin' and snorin'

Like an easterly wind on the back end
Of a northern blizzard.

Several of the men reared up
To go to the rescue of Carlita.
They bestrode their horses and cussed
'Neath their breath, "Destiny or death"—
For determined was they to get back
The lass they adored,
For what was Abilene without Carlita's amour?
Finally, they neared the bungalow,
And dismounted so as not to alert the rascal inside
Of his impending doom
(They could see from a distance,
There was at least one candle lit).
Two went to the side of the house
And three or so snuck to the back,
And four were at the front, ready to attack.
And on the count of three,
They battered the doors before
The fool inside could get his suspenders
Up around his shoulder.
For surely surprised was he
By this daring rescue of Carlita Lee.

"Gents," called he, "ne'er meant no harm—
But this here's a gal who can charm.
I was caught up in her spell
And just couldn't see
How to live my life
Without Miss Carlita Lee.
Don't! Don't hurt me none," he cried,
"'Cause I'm purity dang sure
You'd do the same thang,

If you'd thought it first."
And with that said,
He attempted to bolt.
But, with a leap and a thrust
The men beat him and bound him
To the floor.
When the dust settled,
Someone realized Carlita
Was nowhere in sight.
They searched in the other room and found
Their sweetheart still in doom:
Hands tied behind her back,
She lay across the rumpled sheets,
The gunnysack still o'er her head.

Someone lifted it and cut the ropes.
She gasped, and then she smiled.
"Why, fellas," said she in her familiar way,
"I was a' wonderin'
Whether you's gonna rescue me today!
Sure good to see the lot of you.
What ya say we mosey
On o'er to O'shay Bar
And kick up some dust?
I gotta tell ya, you done me proud!
Why, I wanna tell everyone—fer cryin' out loud!"

And at that, one of 'em bellowed
"Carlita Lee, we'll always keep you free
To go wherever you may.
'Cause we feel you tuggin'
At our heartstrings
With your yearnin' to roam.
Why Carlita, you is our butterfly.

Jest remember us fellers today
In your kindly way."

Po' women of Abilene
Just sigh and keep a-moanin'
Bearin' as best they can
With Carlita's way,
And the love-struck men
That carried on that day.
Folks, I hear tell that ev'ry now and again
A peculiar wind blows through Abilene
And men commence to swaggerin'
As though love-smitten.
For Carlita's spirit preys upon the land,
A wanderin' forever free
Givin' her kind of love,
Always so generously!

## Ain't No Romance

Ain't quite figured the attraction of the West,
Where many bemoan the romance,
The adventure, and the rest.

For what is it really? All that I can see
Is an opportunity granted to live in liberty.

Ain't no panacea, or utopia and such,
Just some forward thinkin'
That's convinced slavery is too much.

So I could roam in freedom
In Texas, Alabama, and New Mexico,
Long as I could toil and frolic in any season.

Ain't no romance for me,
Just a journey to be free.

## All Hail to Cowhands—Our Friends

All hail to the cowhands,
For kindred spirits are we:
Evaluatin' life's prospects here and there,
Tryin' to make sense of the complexities
We see everywhere.
For one thing we glean,
As we gallop by the way,
We each have pieces to the puzzle
We define as livin' from day to day.

And once this journey is ended,
And we gather from near and far,
Finally, we'll see the pieces together,
Realizin' that in each other
And beyond what we could know,
Are the rationales for life's peaks
And the valleys trudged below.

And as we sit along the hillsides,
And ponder on the way
What essentially are life's lessons
We garner from day to day;
Whether it be ropin' or bulldoggin',
Each twist in the bend
Broadens our comprehension
Of the mystery of being human.

# SECTION FOUR
## Our Values—
## A Cowboy Life Perspective

# A Blank Page

Can't write my story;
All I know is to say,
Ain't nothin' you do
That I didn't do better
At the end of yesterday.

I'd hog-tied the best of 'em
And bull dogged the rest of 'em.
I'm certain, fact is,
I'm mighty sure,
Ain't none y'all out there
That can keep my score.

I ain't braggin'—facts is facts,
I'm heralded in this here cow-punchin',
And that's that.
I done bronc-busted more'n y'all ever will see,
Or read, or hear
On that box called TV.

My tale ain't in no book, and rightly so;
It's spoken from heart to heart
For all to know.
I done blazed many a trail from Oregon
Down through Kansas
And across the Texas dale.
My hands done got blistered
Worse'n my feet
From ropin' them broncs
And chasin' 'em beyond the streets.

And yep, ev'ry now 'n again
I'd lose sight of a couplea bulls;
But 'fore you'd be a tattlin',
I'd done found the critters that gone astray.
All I do, is jus' rescue 'em from Hell's center
And lead 'em to graze
Where the bramble bush is thinner.

Not much to say 'bout this here life, but a
Powerful lot to do.
I jus thank the good Lawd,
Ev'ry day and night—
He gave me a heap o' fortitude.

Yep, I done my part,
And the part of others, too;
Did all I know'd
I was s'posed to do.
Ain't no sense carryin' on;
History didn't leave me a page, but
Don't make no ne'er mind to me—
Like I done told you,
I was the best cowhand y'all ever did see.

# Our Story

Does anyone care about the legacy
That tells our story
Wrested from the annals of mankind?
Does anyone care that we still feel
All the suffering we experienced
On the journey, from the start?

Who will cast a caring eye,
Or ensure the tale is told:
The romance, the adventure,
And the disappointment on the road?

Who will let fall a compassionate tear
That trickles into oceans and rivers
And roars with the anguish
Of generations dwelling in servitude?
Who will care whether we are remembered
In our beauty, our ugliness, our essence?

Who will remain objective,
Irrespective of the display?
Of hurt, harm, and danger
Suffered along the way?

Don't know what will be
As a consequence of our history;
Will we find a different space
Where the stones in the foundation
And the bricks in the walls
Evolve from God's eternal grace?

Will we be able to shed light
On a new start
Written from the expressions
Of what life does impart?

So let's gather together
And relinquish chains that bind.
For the essence of life
Is to evolve and grow,

Move to a new place
Where parity we find.

Does anyone care what lies beyond?
At least there's you and me.
We seek what's expressed herein
That makes us unique and free.

So let's take it upon ourselves
To deliberate further
How the tale gets told,
To discover a way,
Alone and unparalleled,
Where truth will forever resound.

Don't know, I admit; 'tis disconcerting
Our lives aren't really in our hands;
But we must ponder on what's so true:
There's a Creator who orchestrates the Plan.

## Movin' On

Lyin' on my back in the sage brush,
My hand as a pillow for my head,
I was gazin' into the wispy clouds
Ponderin' what I'd come to dread.

I had to leave here soon,
My youth ground to dust;
No matter what it seem I do,
Just can't make a buck.

Gotta go where I can eke out a livin'.
Only one more dream to chase;

No sense lingerin' here—
Aint nothin' left to trust in this place.

Gotta go where I can gallop
Freely through the countryside
And hammer out what is meant
By living on the rough side.

I'll stop and work a spell,
'Til time to move on again.
And I'll contemplate God's blessings,
Remembering all the places I've been.

Must go where I can be free
To work this mighty land—
Someplace where my spirit can soar
As an industrious cowhand.

I' ain't wantin' to deal with papers
And businessmen and such;
Just let me wander where I may—
No claims to the land, not wantin' much

Except the touch of sunrise and the glimmer of sunset,
Perhaps just a hint of wind and rain
Just to clear things out a bit as I start off again,
Askin' only for respite on God's terrain.

## My Cowboy Persona

I have never been a cowhand,
Although I wonder if I had been
What I would have been like
On the prairie way back then.

I suspect I'd be
More of the timid type.
Afraid of snakes,
And scared to sleep
On the ground at night.

If I had encountered rough,
Ruthless men,
I would have cowered in my boots
From sheer fright of them.
Of course, I wager a mean streak
Would rise up now and then,
As I lasso any flippant louse
Who cheated me at cards,
Stole my whiskey, or spilled my gin.

But on the serene side
Is the yearning
To know other cowhands
That like what I like.
Those kindred spirits
Who marvel at a sunrise and a sunset
And are roused by hard rains
That leave one soaking wet
But clean of scum, dust, and mildew.

Those sensitive souls
Who enjoy the constellations,
And hum tunes beyond lullabies;
Who appreciate the simple things:
The centipede that crosses over
Rather than take a bite,
Or a crackling good fire
That warms the bones on a chilly night.

Nay, many more things than these
Would certainly put my heart at ease
If I hung out on the range.
Back then with compatriots
Who would swagger and sway
As the tales we'd swap would
Get as long as the day,
As we leaned back hard
Against any post or tree
With a chaw and a straw
And revel in stories of the prairie.

Traveling long and riding hard,
With calloused hands and blistered feet
From tasks seemingly endless to complete:
Would I have murmured and complained
Because there was no end
To grueling tasks?
In the face of danger would I stand tall,
Or would I high-tail it out of harm's way
In a flash?

Would I have been the gruff
But good, hardy type?
Acclimated to hard work
And fair treatment
In spite of the hell one would pay
For being one of the good guys—
Come what may?
Would I have been respected
For my joviality
And willingness to lend a hand,
Wherever the need?

Or would I have been foolhardy
And disdained for cowardice and shady deeds?

Tough to imagine
What I would have been
As a cowhand on the range
Way back then.
But, this one thing I hold to be true:
I would have had a grand time
No matter what I would do,
Or despite what some would say—
For a hardworking, frolicking cowhand
Would be my true way!

# The Big Chore

I reckon contemplating life as a big chore
Don't make it any easier for some
To get about their business
Doin' what needs to be done.

Nay, it makes more sense to me
With all this buckin' and jivin'
To cast life as one big rodeo,
We all doin' whatever we can for survivin'.

Oh, some of us will hold on
At least a spell or two;
Others, as soon as they hit the saddle,
Will bust their way right through;

But what matters
In the end
Is the perspective you put on it

As you round the bend.

'Cause no matter whether it be
A chore to you, or a rodeo ride,
We've all got to journey through it,
In our own stride.

## A Prairie Illusion

I was alone on the prairie, under the stars one night
Watching fireflies chase each other gleaming with delight,
While as intensely I gazed,
My eyes saw something to amaze:

Where once there were fireflies
Now appeared children beneath the starry sky!
They laughed, sang, chased each other 'round—
They even tried to wrestle one another to the ground!

I marveled at their love, at their laughter and delight
And wondered, why can it never be the human plight
To jostle and to hug, and to lose the veneer
That is worn when a stranger comes too near?

Why can it not be the human plight
To enjoy each other's company rather than fuss and fight,
To chase fireflies like glittering dreams in children's play,
To spend more time in laughter throughout the day?

Why can it not be the ambition of men
To exemplify the generosity of the spirit within,
And let involvement show only courtesy,
And to gracious activities bring lovely harmony?

As I gazed upon the children that day
Across the prairie happily engaged in play,
Like a flitter before my very eyes,
They metamorphosed into glittering fireflies.

## My Value

Is there merit in being ranked
A little lower than angels, higher than dogs,
When it comes to bustin' stallions,
Herding cattle, or sloppin' hogs?
Should I feel proud I'm placed higher
Than a horse? So says my master,
Who won't let me break 'em
Lest there be a disaster.

Well, if earnin' a livin'
Is what its about
Then I wanna be toilin'
Where there's the most clout.
Some would say ain't no disrespect
In any kind of work.
A man should ne'er be afraid
To scratch a livin' from the dirt!

But I 'spect it's okay to be particular
'Bout what you put your hand to
If'n you wanna enjoy
The kinfolk who surround you!
And to the desperados,
Stop riskin' limb or life
Just earn an honest livin'—
Don't matter if you ain't got no wife.

I'm a seekin a toilin' that's gonna keep me
Safe as long as I am able—
My kin are fed and clothed
As they sit 'round my table.
The other day, overseer got to yakkin'
'Bout wantin' us'n to bust
Some stallions he seen along the way
All kickin' up the dust.

Master said, "It'll wipe out my investment.
These negras cost a thousand each, man.
I ain't ready to see 'em dead, or busted up,
'Cause they out breakin' stallions!
Got other tasks in mind for 'em to do,
Like herdin' cattle and balin' hay;
Ain't givin' up nary one of 'em
To work 'em stallions like you say."

Nah, ain't as high as angels;
Guess I'm higher than them dogs
When it come to herdin' cattle,
Pickin' cotton, or sloppin' hogs.
But one thing I swear
I learned it to be true:
I'm higher than some stallions
In my master's view!

So, I eke out my livin'
Content with the claim
That I work free from harm
And I work free from shame.

At the end of a week on the trail,
Or at the end of a day balin' hay,

I come home to my folk,
And know that my work ain't no joke.

Shucks, got a bit of respect too, 'cause
Master claims he won't risk my life or limb
Bustin' stallions as a livin' for him,
Knowin' this makes me grin!

## A Perspective

From where I'm a sittin'
There's a mighty heap of chores and tears.
Yet dispersed betwixt heartaches
Are delights that calm most fears.

You must love the sunrise,
Irrespective of how gloomy the rest of the day.
And, ya gotta love the frolic of carefree livin'
That comes now and again your way.

And beyond the disappointment
Of unrewarded toil and chance
Is the conviction that the life you be a livin'
Can really be a romance.

From where I'm a sittin'
Most things don't end up
In world-wide acclaim
But if you are willing, truly focused—

If you can grasp onto the brass
And do your best in everything,
Then you'll have reaped a richer place
That peacefulness and thanksgiving brings.

# A Cowboy's Holiday Wish

Besides being tucked in a warm, snug place
Away from the bitin' cold and the cowhand's pace
It would be nice to see others feelin' merry
When they think of me.

And why not? I'm a cowhand;
Earn my keep doin' what I do.
As I done told many, it's an honest livin',
Herdin' cattle among sagebrush the whole year through.

All right; I admit a lonely spell or two.
Is there anyone out there betwixt hither and yon
That'll wish this ole cowhand a merry Christmas
And happiness beyond?

Especially at Christmas when there ain't that much to do,
I get to wishin' to occupy some space
Where there's a lonely heart to be brightened
By the sight of my ol' whiskered face.

And what's wrong wid wishin' for a little mistletoe
To brighten other folks wid a glimpse of my livin'?
It's jest a caretaker's passion,
To be rid gloom in a more lively fun lovin' fashion!

Some may find it delightful to hear me spin a yarn
'Bout the ways of a cowhand throughout the year,
When bustin' stallions and ropin' longhorns
Is all that we hold dear.

So, I'm a wishin' upon yonder star
That 'em angels I see a' wanderin' near and far

Will pause a minute or two,
And sprinkle stardust upon you.

## Ere New Year's

Here it is near the witching hour.
Shall I mull over what lies ahead?
Surely if I do, I'll conjure up
Unnecessary evils to dread.
Nay, let me lay in this place
Near the embers of a quiet fire,
Where larks echo in the ether,
Where silence meets the stars.

Nay let me rest—just sit a spell—
With my hat pulled o'er my face,
Just reveling in God's good grace.
Got lots to be grateful for:
The new moon, the rise of a new day,
Averting the danger that lurks
Along a trailblazer's way.

Is this what I have come to face,
Blazing cattle trails?
The ins and outs, the 'twixt and 'tweens
Of nature's perplexing wails?
How dare I ask for more, you say?
Oh ye of little faith!
When above me looms the endless sky,
And around me prevails His grace!

Nay, let me lie upon this patch o' land
Not far from the calming sea
And be thankful in my cowboy heart

That He cares for even me.
God's been good,
Mighty good, it seems,
To a wanderer whose days are filled
With the dust of idle dreams.

## The New West?

The need to roam—
Is it really new?
To yield to the urge
Like a cowboy true
And lay in prairie grass,
Gazing into a puffy sky
While daydreaming
As life passes by?

The dream within our cowboy's heart
To venture where others ne'er tread
And leave our very own imprints
Of carefree-living widely spread?
Or heed the pounding of our runaway heart
To blaze trails like yesteryear
Where we rectify tales of ancestors
Saying it wasn't all fun-filled cheer.

And what is the wilderness
We long to cross
As a cowboy saddled
On a dappled-gray horse?
Discovery and adventure mask
Inherent desires of lofty ambition
For our urge to recreate
Beyond the stretches of imagination.

Is it really new,
This place where instinctively we strive
Through wildly acclaimed adventure
To inspire as well as to survive?
This wilderness of exploration
Espouses the liberty to pursue
Anything we deem important, and
Whatever we choose creatively to do.

## Last Meal

Rippling rivers run
Along high, haughty hills
Speckled by streaks of searing sun.

And throughout this rugged region,
Dashing daringly across the plain,
Are lean longhorn steer by the legion.

Chased by ravenous, raging coyotes
Seeking to slake their famine
By the slaughter of several hundred of these.

Alert to arms, but failing to avert the fateful feast,
They falter and fall
As the entrée for these willful beasts.

## Beyond Corrals

Like bucking broncos
Stomping limitations
And seizing expectations,
They yelp and break onto the field

After slumber.

Exploding with merriment,
Hands hooked in anticipation
For undaunted exploration
Where fantasy and dreams unite
In new wonders affixed in a child's delight.

## Assumptions Don't 'Mount to Nothin'

On a continuum from point A to infinity
Lotta folk perplexed by this mystery:
The wonderment of success,
Whether there's a link to happiness.

Since I spend most my time in gaiety
Ain't nothin' 'bout life gonna bother me.
'Cause I reckon I pass this way but once—
I got plenty o' dreams to unravel before Eternity's done!

If I ain't figgered it out betwixt
Now and then, I reckon
I got rather a go of it,
So I'll give it another spin.

Ain't messed wit' nobody,
Ain't stirrin' da pot,
Ain't down on my luck,
'Cause it matters not:

For I keep on as I round the bend,
And if twirlin's my appointed place
I'll keep on twirlin' to my journey's end—
Won't shudder 'bout being a disgrace.

How can anyone truly define
Whether this life here I've lived
Among a heap of mankind
Is a wasted life of mine?

Indeed, others will write my epitaph
To categorize their spin,
But their assumptions don't mount to nothin'
'Cept to leave me a-grinnin'!

# Horse and Man

Some say riding in a saddle
Countless hours on a horse
Means intimacy with more than cattle:
It's like love that runs its course.

Cattle runs are long and hard,
And can weary one to the bone,
But if you get your saddle right,
It's like sitting on a throne.

Because you and your horse progress
And the exchange betwixt the two
As an indomitable force
Becomes familiar to you.

Much like a lover,
Your partner on the trail
Who was first your long-time friend
Comes to know you in every veil.

During the good moods
As well as all the bad,
Your horse becomes
The best lover you ever had.

He recognizes your gait
And he understands your howl
That'll carry him along
For many a mile.

Like sweethearts in nuptial bliss,
You treasure his present readiness;
He accommodates your every move,
Relishing tender pats of pleasantness.

An in-depth affinity grows
As you explore each other's forms;
For what evolves through cattlery,
Are new discoveries surprisingly born.

After miles and miles of prairie,
Of grueling, endless trail runs,
When, fatigued, you lose your compass,
And rely on your horse's hum;

Or during the times when sick,
In the saddle, feverish and blue,
Your horse at those times
Knows instinctively what to do.

Thus, trust that evolves for a horseman
Keeps you safe, near and far,
Where sensitivity and unity
Are sanctioned by the stars.

# What's Lovely

*"…Whatsoever things are true,*
*whatsoever things are honest,*
*whatsoever things are pure,*
*whatsoever things are lovely,*
*whatsoever things are of good report;*
*if there be any virtue,*
*and if there be any praise,*
*think on these things." Philippians 4:8*

To use the gifts that are given,
To walk in the manner that's best,
To handle all life's challenges through
The confidence of God's perfection
In the test,
Is to ponder carefully,
Perplexity
In the mysterious way it un-bounds
And thread the intrigue into ribbons of delight
Where the purity of love is a respite
From unkind sights.

# Transporter's Honor

What honor it brings
To be the mechanism
To which this life form clings—

Destined to come from afar
To fulfill a mission
Prescribed in the stars.

Yet duties that entail
Until this life form comes of age
Require guidance to prevail,

To follow the path, to experience
The beauty and shared vision
That adds value to this existence

Described as living.

## An Airy Lullabye

As I ponder stars above,
Countless in the sky,
Will one fall upon my head
And whisper a lullabye?

Little do the stars above
Know more than my name.
It would be spectacular
If they had more to gain.

How splendid it would feel
If only one I could claim
As my star, my special star
I would quietly proclaim.

So light upon me, shiny bright,
And hear my weary plea.
For crossin' this vast terrain
Has made me so lonely.

# Well Run Dry

Ain't nothin' left to pull up.
Dug deep, eons and eons ago;
Is this an indicator done reached the peak?
Ain't nothin' more to know?

Done cast far and wide into the abyss.
The only sound that echoes
'Gainst hollow winds
Is scrapin' and scratchin' for inspiration.

Only thing remains to question:
Is it done in the way it must be?
Or is there some finite chance
There may be more to see?

Some'll say, "You are free to cast
Any particular opinion aside;
Release yourself, and just be,
Done finally hit your stride."

"Time's come to float amongst the clouds;
Yet, your soul does speak:
It held too long to somber dreams;
Fantasy has met its peak."

Alas, the burden of the soul,
Anchored and forlorn,
Chained to the pits of hell,
Ne'er to be mourned.

No self-pity going' on,
Wistful moments sigh,

'Tis what 'tis—and what is done.
The well is simply dry!

## An Accountin'

A fragile thing, this life of ours;
How it ebbs and flows.
Ideals intended to pursue
And promises meant to keep
Ere the whistle blows
A-callin' to eternal sleep.

Will we ever wonder, then,
What prevented us from livin'
When capacity and capability were
Ours to create?
Yet, somehow, permitted we
Others our destiny to shape.

Is there perchance an opportunity
To couple circumstance with hindsight
And latent wisdom,
To re-create a wholesome state
And a quality life
All worth livin'?

Woefully, do we see how time escapes to eternity,
Where we shall be summoned
To the terms of accountability?
And when shall we speak
Of intentions weak, and
Will failed mightily?

To follow destiny's call,
To prevail on purpose's trail,
In our role to humanity?
Woe that we must face
What we failed to do
To leave this world a better place
For others destined to pass through.

# I Thought It Was Gonna Be Different

I thought it was gonna be different
Out here in the West, under the open sky.
I thought I'd get respected for doing my best
Workin' as a cowhand
Along the Mexico-Oregon trail,
Risking danger to limbs and loss of health;
I thought I'd acquire respect and great wealth.

*Au contraire*—this reality
For the quest for freedom
And respectability
Still eludes me; even as a hired hand,
There is no acknowledgment
That I am a man, a creature with a soul,
And yearnings to be treated whole.

As I wander through this dirt and dust and grime,
Bulldoggin', cattle herdin',
And takin' on any kind of gig I can find,
I long to wander upon a place
Where the air is crisp and breathing is free,
To stumble upon the trail that leads to respectability.

Until then, I will forlornly roam
This dismal earth 'til I'm called home.
And I will ask the Taskmaster on that day
What was the meaning of sufferin' in this way?
For my hands and my feet
Shall bear the imprint of defeat.
The failure of a thirst unquenched—
A dream squelched by intolerance stench.

## Meditation

A-travelin' to Santa Fe,
The windin', dusty trail,
Twisted I around distant points,
A-climbin' sundry hills,
Seeking the vertex of dreams afar
While discovering pathways
To destiny's star.

I poked hither and prodded yon
Among the varied peaks,
Attempting to view dawn's best days
'Twixt these mysterious peaks.
Paused I to cast my glance upon misty skies,
Ribboned with swirls of orange and pink.
Here, thought I, is where daybreak winks.

A-travelin' to Santa Fe,
Destined was I to glean
A chorus echoed melodiously,
Interspersed with the coyotes refrain.
Here, grinned I, is where eagles reign
And vigor is restored again.
Chuckled I, now and then.

I dipped my sombrero in cool streams
Running casually over rocks,
Reprieving me of yesterday's groans
When work was so hard.
Pondered I with earnestness,
The essence of escapades
That leave one breathless.

And, as I gazed upon this place,
The winding Santa Fe Trail
That embraces the worn;
Serenity's cloak,
Gathered to bless
And beckoned me to succumb
To its pinnacle of happiness.

## The Whisper of the Wind

It's good sometimes
To hear the quiet wind
Prompting, gently urging us
To relish the silence within.
And that is what will happen

If you ride as long as I do
In the open of the day;
Then with the stars at the close
You come to appreciate
The repose of a quiet soul.

I invite you to contemplate
How tranquility can restore you,
As you traverse life's path;

Oh, listen to the whisper of the wind
Beckoning you to let
Serenity become your friend.

## Where Angels Play

Perched against a wagon wheel,
Ponder I about this place.
The Good Book says
It's where angels descend and ascend,
Afore the morning dew cascades
And a purplish haze fills the space.

Is this the place
Where cherubs come to play
And disperse laughter among cotton clouds,
Gold harps strapped to their wings
That flutter from gentle winds
And bring merriment to the forlorn?

Is this the place
Where dewdrops moisten eyelids
Against the glaring sun,
Where will-o-the-wisps on the breeze
Float gently past
As katydids begin their tasks?

Perhaps this is the place
Where silence entices dreams
To scamper in the weight
Of the morning light
And forbid review of
Yesterday's plight?

Just must be the place
Where angels flick whispers
Of delight
In the ears of weary men
Who through the sense of destiny
Are on this trail again.

# About the Author

Sharon's origins as a writer began in her years at Claude Chester Elementary School in Groton, CT, where she spent her free time writing stories and reading extensively. It was her way of separating herself from her feelings of alienation, low self-esteem, and the stigma associated with being a foster child, a "ward of the state." When she graduated from grade school, her teacher presented her with a large package of the stories she had submitted for his review. His encouraging words to  her communicated that one day, he believed, she would be recognized for her creative writing.

Years later, Sharon sought to get acclimated to Georgia's culture after she and her husband moved from Alabama. Her husband was still employed in Alabama for several months while she had begun work at her new job in Georgia. At some point, Sharon read in the newspaper about a poetry society and decided to write poems for the review so as to become eligible for membership (and thus build relationships). Her poetry was well received; she was interviewed by Joel Hayes, founder of Douglas County's Poetry Writers Group. During the interview, Joel invited her to write and present a poem at a Cowboy Gathering event. Although she was stunned that she was asked to read a poem out loud—at the time, she believed poems were best suited to silent reading—her poem "A Cowboy Persona" was a hit!

Sharon soon became a performing artist at the Fourth, Fifth, and Sixth Annual Georgia Cowboy Gatherings. According to the *Douglas Journal Sentinel*, "Sharon's unique style brings an African American perspective on western cowboy poetry. She weaves tales of African American contributors as well as captures the essence of the western *esprit de corps* through her unique, engaging style".

Joel Hayes; Charlie Holloway, author of *Ol' Saddles & Good Advice*; and many listeners repeatedly encouraged Sharon to write a cowboy poetry book. Her research indicated the history of African American cowboys was not widely known. Hence, she created poetry designed not only for entertainment, but also to convey a historic viewpoint. The perspective aims to usher the reader and the audience into the experience through an empathetic, vivid imaginary exchange incurred during the struggle to live free, to be treated as a viable citizen, to retain family relationships, to improve the quality of life for family and for others, and to simply enjoy the cowboy lifestyle.

Sharon was prompted to move forward with the publication of the book to enable creation of a poetic legacy, and to leverage funding to meet her aspiration of enabling "aged out" girls to develop enriching lifestyles that will prepare them for self-sufficiency as adults. She attributes the talent God has blessed her with and her commitment to live a godly life as the underlying factor of her success. She states emphatically, "And we know that all things work together for good to them that love God, to them who are the called according to His purpose." (Romans 8:28 KJV) Sharon currently resides in Wisconsin with her husband, James, and her younger daughter, Jamie. Her older daughter, Tylene, is married and also lives in Wisconsin with two daughters, Mekayla and Noelle.

# Bibliography

Bolden, Tonya. *The Book of African-American Women: 150 Crusaders, Creators and Uplifters.* Mass: Adams Media Corporation, 1996 (reprint 2004).

Cox, Clinton. *The Forgotten Heroes: The Story Of The Buffalo Soldiers.* New York: Scholastic Paperbacks, 1996.

Hassrick, Royal B. *Cowboys, The Real Story of Cowboys and Cattlemen.* London: Octopus Books, 1974.

Pinkney, Andrea D. Bill Pickett, *Rodeo-Ridin Cowboy.* San Diego: Gulliver Books, Harcourt Brace & Co., 1996.

Schlissel, Lillian. *Black Frontiers, A History of African American Heroes in the Old West.* New York: Simon & Schuster, 1995.

Sherr, Lynn and Jurate Kazickas. *Susan B. Anthony Slept Here: A Guide to American Women's Landmarks.* New York: Times Books, 1994.

Smith, Jessie C. *Epic Lives: One Hundred Black Women Who Made A Difference.* Michigan: Visible Ink Press, 1993.

Tucker, Phillip T. *Cathy Williams: From Slave to Female Buffalo Soldier.* Pennsylvania: Stackpole Books, 2009.

**Websites:**

Bridget "Biddy" Mason - Distinguished Women of Past and Present. http://www.distinguishedwomen.com/biographies/mason-b.html (October 27, 2001)

Buffalo Soldiers History, U.S. Indian and Span-Am Wars. www.ushist. com/buffalo-soldiers.htm

The Buffalo Soldiers a historical view. www.sru.edu/depts/scc/ collaborate/pages/buffalos/polk.html

The Buffalo Soldiers on the Western Frontier. www.imh.org/imh/buf/ buf6.html